mindful
LEARNING

DR CRAIG HASSED is an internationally recognised expert in mindfulness who has presented widely at national and international seminars and conferences and has published extensively in the areas of mind–body medicine and mindfulness. He has been instrumental in promoting mindfulness as a simple, natural and accessible technique for enhancing wellness, preventing and managing illness, and improving performance within health, educational and corporate settings. Craig is a senior lecturer and mindfulness consultant at Monash University, and co-author of Exisle's very successful *Mindfulness for Life*.

DR RICHARD CHAMBERS is a clinical psychologist in private practice, where he specialises in mindfulness-based therapies and runs regular mindfulness courses. He is also employed as a mindfulness consultant by Monash University and regularly consults to top-tier law firms and premier educational institutions. Richard is actively involved in research, has published a number of peer-reviewed articles and has presented at a number of academic conferences. He is also a developer of Smiling Mind, a free web and iPhone app designed to make mindfulness accessible to young people.

DR CRAIG HASSED &
DR RICHARD CHAMBERS

mindful
learning

Reduce stress and improve brain

performance for effective learning

EXISLE
PUBLISHING

First published 2014

Exisle Publishing Pty Ltd
'Moonrising', Narone Creek Road, Wollombi, NSW 2325, Australia
P.O. Box 60–490, Titirangi, Auckland 0642, New Zealand
www.exislepublishing.com

National Library of Australia Cataloguing-in-Publication Data:

Hassed, Craig, author.

Mindful learning : reduce stress and improve brain performance for effective learning /
Dr Craig Hassed & Dr Richard Chambers.

ISBN 978 1 921966 39 2

Includes bibliographical references and index.

Mental efficiency.
Attention.
Consciousness.
Thought and thinking.

Chambers, Richard, author.

153

Designed by Christabella Designs
Typeset in Bembo 11.5/18
Printed in Shenzhen, China, by Ink Asia

This book uses paper sourced under ISO 14001 guidelines from
well-managed forests and other controlled sources.

10 9 8 7 6 5 4 3

DISCLAIMER

While this book is intended as a general information resource and all care has been taken in
compiling the contents, this book does not take account of individual circumstances and is
not in any way a substitute for professional advice. Neither the author nor the publisher and
their distributors can be held responsible for any loss, claim or action that may arise from
reliance on the information contained in this book.

CONTENTS

Introduction: What is education?   1

1. What is mindfulness?   5

2. The science of mindfulness   21

3. Stress, focus and performance   35

4. Why attention matters   43

5. Applied mindfulness   49

6. Sharpening the tool   57

7. Learning, mental flexibility and problem solving   67

8. Mindsets and learning   77

9. Resilience and managing stress   85

10. Emotional development   97

11. Communication and relationships   103

12. eMindfulness   115

13. Enhancing creativity   121

14. Movement and sport   131

15. Teaching with attention   141

16. Working with resistance   151

17. Managing personal stress in the classroom   159

18. Mindfulness beyond the classroom   169

19. Organisational approaches to mindfulness   191

20. The exercises   199

Endnotes   239

Index   247

INTRODUCTION
What is education?

Why start a book on education and learning with a question to which the answer is seemingly so obvious that it hardly needs asking? Well, perhaps education, in the true sense of the word, isn't what we generally take it to be. The English word 'education' comes from the Latin word *educare* which means 'to draw forth, to bring out, elicit, develop' implying there is intuitive knowledge or wisdom within the individual that can be uncovered through a process of observation, inquiry and reflection on experience.[1]

In this approach to education, the teacher is there to facilitate or draw out insight by engaging attention and encouraging inquiry and questioning. Potential knowledge resides within the student and the flow of knowledge is from the inside-out, with the teacher helping the student to discern the value or relevance of what comes forth. In fact, we can learn from any situation and so the whole world and every moment is potentially our teacher.

This inside-out approach to education is at least as old as the ancient Greeks. This is what the 'Socratic method' or dialectic approach was all about. If we openly and objectively look at what is in front of us and ask the right questions we will discover how things are for ourselves and not just because we are told what to think. Mindful education is entirely sympathetic with this inquiring approach.

Much of what is called education in the modern day is more about providing information and knowledge from the outside, i.e. instructing the student in a body of knowledge which the teacher imparts and the student absorbs like a sponge. From the student's perspective the flow of knowledge is from the outside-in; this is not 'to draw forth' but rather 'put in'. The knowledge at which this approach aims is more akin to doctrine, information, beliefs and opinions, not wisdom or insight. Providing information, of course, has its place but if that is all education is then we will have left out the most important and interesting part of learning, the part that makes the world a fascinating place, that encourages self-reliance and personal growth, and that taps into the core of our being. These two approaches to education are not mutually exclusive and one's experience at school, university or in one's job will probably have been a mixture of them.

This book, however, is dedicated to education based on mindfulness — learning from 'within', education as 'drawing out', and knowledge as 'wisdom'. Such an approach is underpinned by awareness and openness. It is not just about our approach to formal education but also about learning in the 'school of life'. This approach is not opposed to education as we commonly think of it, it just starts from a different premise and looks with a larger perspective.

The mindful approach to education is eminently practical for preparing us for a fulfilling personal and professional life. It will help us to better understand and remember, to better manage stress and organise ourselves. It can also help us to be happier, more engaged with the community and, importantly, to find learning as interesting as it should be. To quote the twentieth-century writer and philosopher, Gilbert Chesterton: 'There are no uninteresting things, only uninterested people.'

When learning becomes reduced to merely cramming away information and regurgitating it for exams, it somewhat loses the fascination that was natural to us as a young child. It is of this kind of education that Albert Einstein said, 'Education is what remains after one has forgotten everything he learned in school'. Einstein managed to maintain that child-like fascination throughout the whole of his life. If we are a parent or teacher, the challenge is how to help children stay interested and not to 'snuff out the candle' due to the type of education we received.

> *The fairest thing we can experience is the mysterious. It is the fundamental emotion which stands at the cradle of true art and true science. He who knows it not and can no longer wonder, no longer feel amazement, is as good as dead, a snuffed-out candle.*
>
> Albert Einstein

If we don't look, if we don't pay attention, then we don't see what's there, we don't get interested, we don't learn and, what is even sadder, we don't find things interesting. If we pay attention to the world around us we may discover the things that stared others in the face also but that they just didn't see. It's all about having your eyes open. If they're not open, if we're not really looking, then the world is a far less interesting place and we will learn little other than believing what we're told to believe whether it has real merit or not.

Einstein also felt that real discovery was an intuitive process. 'Intuition' — another interesting word — comes from the Latin word *intueri*, meaning to look upon, consider, contemplate. Intuition, in its real meaning, is not what many people take it to be — merely an unconscious, unreflecting, conditioned or automatic way of seeing things. It is all about being conscious and aware. If we really look we have a chance of understanding, because that which is within us is connecting with what we are observing. Thus connectedness, or unity, goes hand in hand with learning mindfully.

•

This book is drawn from a number of important sources including:
- the rapidly expanding body of research on mindfulness
- the world's great wisdom traditions
- years of experience as mindfulness practitioners
- personal experience.

We believe that all these sources have an important contribution to make as they complement and reinforce each other. It is really up to you, the reader, to explore, question, reflect and discover for yourself what works and what doesn't. The journey to becoming a mindful teacher and learner is a lifelong project.

Mindfulness exercises

Importantly, this book is not just about the theory of mindfulness, it is about the practice and experience of it. Theory without experience is like surface learning without real understanding. To that end, there are a number of practical mindfulness exercises or experiments provided in Chapter 20. These are as much for the benefit of the one who seeks to learn mindfulness as well as for the one who wishes to teach it in the classroom or at home. They can be used as scripts or, even better, once you become familiar with them you can guide these exercises in your own words. References throughout the book will direct you to the relevant exercise.

CHAPTER 1

What is mindfulness?

If the first question was 'What is education?' then the second has to be 'What is mindfulness?' because, after all, this is a book about mindful education. Mindfulness is both old and new: old in the sense that the world's great wisdom traditions have used various meditative or contemplative practices for millennia; and new in the sense that the world has all of a sudden 'discovered' mindfulness. Over the last ten to twenty years there has been a veritable explosion of research on mindfulness-based approaches for diverse endeavours such as enhancing mental and physical health, education, sport and leadership training.

The importance of attention is not a new idea. In 1890, William James wrote the first classic textbook on psychology in which he stated:

> *The faculty of voluntarily bringing back a wandering attention over and over again, is the very root of judgment, character and will. No one is* compos sui *[a master of themselves] if he have it not. An education which should improve this faculty would be the education par excellence.*[1]

James recognised the importance of being able to focus attention as the ultimate education and as underpinning the development of 'judgement, character and will'. Unfortunately, by the time James wrote this the West had largely lost touch with contemplative roots, so meditation wasn't widely known about or used. Hence the importance of attention in Western psychology remained largely a footnote for another century, but recently things have changed rather dramatically.

A simple way of defining mindfulness is as *a mental discipline aimed at training attention*. There are also other aspects, for example:

- utilising the senses upon which to train the attention
- engaging the mind in the present moment
- fostering self-control through non-attachment to transitory experiences such as thoughts, feelings and sensations
- encouraging an attitude of openness and acceptance, or being non-judgmental about such transitory experiences
- cultivating equanimity and stillness by being unmoved by, or less reactive to, moment-to-moment experience.

Formally training attention in this way is generally called *mindfulness meditation*. The term meditation can evoke attitudes, assumptions and stereotypical notions. It can also bring with it certain unhelpful expectations, such as being able to 'blank out' one's mind or getting rid of thoughts.

There is nothing particularly Eastern or Western about mindfulness or meditation. The present moment, the mind, the body and attention don't have an east or a west. If we go back to the roots of the words for meditation they refer to 'familiarisation' and 'cultivation'. Through meditation we familiarise ourselves with what *is* rather than the imaginary mental projections and habitual ways of thinking and acting that generally shape and potentially distort experience. Mindfulness cultivates present-moment attention or focus and an attitude of acceptance (rather than reactivity) of moment-by-moment experience. Non-reactivity doesn't mean not responding, it just means that we don't feel compelled to react without choice and discernment.

Paying attention: attention regulation

Mindfulness is not just about meditation; it is also a way of living with awareness. If, for example, we say that a teacher is mindful of a child playing, or a surfer is mindful of the waves, then we mean that he or she is present to whatever is most relevant at that moment and what they are experiencing. 'Attention regulation' is the psychologists' way of saying 'paying attention'. It has a few elements:

- to know where the attention is
- to prioritise where the attention needs to be
- for the attention to go there and stay there.

To know where the attention is

It is surprising how often we are not aware of where our attention is. For example, a student is sitting at his desk 'studying' and then realises he has somehow or other wound up on Facebook again. He didn't see it happen or make a conscious decision to go on Facebook, it just happened 'all by itself'. Another 20 minutes wasted! Another example is a six-year-old child wanting to show her mother something she has made. The mother is mouthing words as if she is interested but is really thinking about how she is going to fit in a whole lot of tasks before going to work. The child knows her mother is not paying attention and says, 'Mummy, loooooook!' Her mother replies, 'I am looking. Yes, that's very interesting dear, now go and put on your shoes.' The child is right, of course — her mother wasn't really looking or listening but she wasn't intentionally telling a lie either because she didn't realise she wasn't really looking. Unconsciously, the child is being taught two things by her mother. First, in order to get an adult's attention you have to make a lot of noise. Second, the parent is modelling inattention and multitasking. Children pick this up early so we shouldn't be surprised that pretty soon they aren't listening to their parents either. Although we may not notice, distraction is happening all the time — when reading, when driving, when watching the television, or when eating.

To prioritise where the attention needs to be

Prioritising where the attention needs to be is an important next step. At any given moment there will be a number one priority as far as our attention is concerned. The priority may change, even in a split second, but at any given moment, when engaged in any activity, there is a central or primary focus for the attention. For example, there might be something very interesting on the radio but when driving the car the attention really needs to be primarily with what's happening on the road. When having a conversation with someone then they are the priority — if they're not then you should excuse yourself and attend to your priority rather than pretending to listen. When a teacher is teaching, the most important thing at that moment is the class. When we're reading an exam paper then that paper is the most important thing. If we don't pay attention we will answer the question we thought we read, which could be very different to the one actually written on the page. Inattention comes at a cost.

For the attention to go there and stay there

For the attention to be focused on what is relevant and to stay there sounds simple, but it's not easy. There are all sorts of things in our internal and external environments competing for our attention. The irrelevant things are 'distracters' and the extent to which they influence focus is known as 'distracter influence'. If we're sitting at our desk studying and find ourselves getting angry because we can't get the attention off the noise coming from the television in the next room, then we are not dealing with distracter influence very well. The more we try to block out distractions, the more our attention goes to them and the more intrusive they are. Attention also gets fixated on the stream of thoughts going through the mind, such as, 'I can't focus' or 'I'm so stupid' or 'I can't stand this' until we can't pay attention to anything but the distraction!

The trick is not to try to block out anything but simply to be more interested in one thing rather than the other. When the attention wanders, as it inevitably will, gently go back to the main priority. If we practise cultivating this during daily meditation then it will be a lot easier to do in our day-to-day life.

Mindfulness in day-to-day life: informal practice

When we're not paying attention the mind slips into what's called 'default mode'. Whether we call it worry, negative self-talk, rumination, daydreaming or simply being away with the birds, this incessant 'thinking' is behind our inability to attend. Mindfulness is not a distraction from our worries. On the contrary: anxiety, negativity, anger and fear are distractions from life. Unless we become aware of the presence and effect of unmindfulness we have little choice about whether or not to engage in it. To be free of it we must first be aware of it.

Mindfulness also implies cultivating an attitude with which we pay attention; one of openness, interest and acceptance. Experience teaches us that when we fight with the thoughts and feelings we would rather not be having we unintentionally feed them with more attention and increase their intrusiveness and impact. Therefore, learning to notice them and be non-reactive to them or non-judgmental about them is an important aspect of learning to be free of them. It's a paradox, but fighting with the stuff we don't like just gets us more deeply mired in it.

To be mindful while eating is to taste the food. To be mindful while having a shower is to feel the water and its warmth. To be mindful while walking is to feel the body moving and to engage with the environment. To be mindful while learning is to pay attention to the teacher and subject matter. To be mindful while teaching is to pay attention to the students. If we start to look closely at what is going on, much of the time we notice that while eating, showering, walking, studying or teaching we are more often than not having a little conversation with ourselves. Worrying, for example, might masquerade as preparation — that is, we might think we are preparing for an exam when actually we are just worrying about how we will go. The problem is, if we practise worrying then we get really good at it and it becomes a habit that is hard to break.

The gateway back into the present moment is through the senses. Although the mind spends a lot of time in the past and the future, the body is only ever in the present moment. The body communicates with the world through the senses, so whenever the mind re-engages with the senses then it is back in touch with the present moment, with reality. This is 'coming to our senses', because it's when we have the opportunity to be a rational, functioning, conscious human being. The formal practice of mindfulness meditation makes this easier to do in day-to-day life.

Mindfulness meditation: formal practice

Mindfulness meditation is sometimes referred to as the formal practice of mindfulness. Meditation is easier if the attention is focused *restfully*. In order to do this you need not struggle with the persistent and distracting stream of circular, habitual, repetitive and imaginary mental activity if it arises. You cannot 'stop the mind from thinking' and any attempt to do so generally leads to heightened tension and frustration. We can, however, learn to be less reactive to it or involved in it. This takes the emotive force out of the thoughts. Many 'trains of thought' come into our minds whether or not we want them to, but we can learn not to be moved by them. It's not a matter of trying to stop them or fight with them, but simply learning that we don't need to get on board any old train of thought that comes into our minds — recognising that any time we find we have boarded a train of thought we can simply get off again. By all means, if you have a useful thought then 'get on the train' after you finish the meditation practice. However, beware: our thoughts have a habit of trying to convince us that they are *all* important.

We give power to whatever our attention is directed to. In giving attention to fearful, anxious, angry or depressing thoughts we are, in a manner of speaking, meditating on them even though they do not serve us well. When we do this, these thoughts become progressively more intrusive, influential and compelling. Furthermore, when we take such imaginings and mental projections to be real then they govern our lives, behaviour and responses to events and, over time, they change brain function, set up stress throughout the body, and accelerate ageing and illness. Worrying about exams, for example, is associated with a significantly increased risk of coming down with an infection during the lead-up to the exam.

Mindfulness meditation is therefore not a method of tuning out but rather tuning in so that after our meditation we might have a better chance of being mindful.

If we are interested in the best results from mindfulness meditation then, paradoxically, we should practise without concern or impatience for the outcome. This is difficult for most people to grasp. We generally come to mindfulness with a certain outcome we would like to achieve — perhaps reduced stress, increased performance or better time management. But expectations take our attention away from the process, reduce acceptance and potentially create tension between our moment-by-moment experience and what we think should be happening. So we have to actually let go of expectations in order to truly practise mindfulness. The more we worry about the outcome, the more we put pressure on ourselves and the more we get in our own way.

A day, or a life for that matter, is just like a book. If it isn't punctuated it becomes a blur and makes little sense. These 'punctuation marks' are times of consciously coming to rest so as to put a little space in the day. The 'full stop' could be practised for anything between 5 and 30 minutes once or, even better, twice a day. How often and how long we practise will depend much on motivation, patience and opportunity. Practising first thing in the morning is useful for being more aware throughout the day. In fact, the biggest predictor of spontaneously mindful moments is previous mindful moments, so meditating first thing makes it much more likely that we will just 'come to our senses' throughout the day. It is best to do this first thing in the morning before getting into the routine of the day. Meditating in the early evening is a great way of letting go of the activity of the day, and to be more present to what is going on in the evening.

A 'comma' in the day can be anything from a couple of seconds to a couple of minutes as often as you remember throughout the day. A comma is particularly useful after having completed one activity and before beginning another. It can add a bit of space, help to reduce the build-up of tension, make us aware of our state of mind and body, and remind us to focus on what comes next.

> Chapter 20, 'The exercises', provides a number of formal mindfulness practices including the full stop and the comma, which you can use and vary according to your needs.

Mindfulness-based cognitive practices

Mindfulness, if we watch closely, can teach us much about how the mind works and what happens when it is not working well. It can provide insight into patterns of thought that are conducive to being happy and functioning well — or the opposite. If we cultivate this insight in our formal practice then we will more quickly notice changes in how we feel and function during the day.

The four main aspects of mindfulness from a cognitive perspective are:
- perception
- non-attachment (letting go)

• acceptance

• present moment.

Perception

A 'stressor' is a situation, event, circumstance or person that triggers our stress or 'fight or flight' response. If, for example, a tiger jumped out of the forest we get ready to run away. That's a pretty useful activation of the fight or flight response. On the other hand, an imaginary stressor will also activate fight or flight if we unmindfully take imagination to be real. Consider, for example, how stressed a student can get over an exam that is weeks away. In reality they could currently be in a completely stress-free environment, but in their imagination they are in a world of pain, imagining the exam, botching up questions, getting imaginary poor exam results, having imaginary conversations with their parents …

To reduce stress mindfully, therefore, is not so much a matter of replacing stress-laden imaginings with falsely positive ones, or arguing with ourselves, or even trying not to have worrying thoughts. What is most important from a mindfulness perspective is to see imagination for what it is — unreal. We cannot be eaten by an imaginary tiger, but we can become afraid and distracted if we think the imaginary tiger is real. Taking imagination to be real is the first distortion of perception that comes with unmindfulness. Reality is easy to deal with compared to the imagination taken to be real. The former we can respond to — get the focus back on studying for the exam, for example. The latter is like fighting with a phantom of our imagination that never gives up.

The next major distortion of perception is to make a 'mountain out of a molehill'. It may be that something is really there but we perceive it to be bigger or more threatening than it really is. To an anxious student, losing a ,mark or two on an assignment might appear to be the end of the world, but in the overall scheme of things it might not be. The mindful remedy is to simply notice what we project onto situations and take an impartial look at the so-called stressor to see if it is really as big as we are making it out to be.

Unmindfully, our thoughts commonly colour or distort the way we see the world and ourselves. A simple comment from someone can, in our mind, be turned in to a major criticism if it's distorted and exaggerated by insecurity and self-criticism. Being on automatic pilot as we often are, we are frequently totally unaware that this whole process is taking place. When we are mindful we only see things as they are.

Non-attachment (letting go)

To relax, mentally or physically, we don't have to 'do anything'. We merely stop holding on. In this sense, mindfulness is about 'non-doing'. Not holding on is called detachment or non-attachment, but these words are often misunderstood. It's not about 'getting rid of', 'cutting off from', 'dissociating from', or 'denying' anything. It's about not being bound to whatever it is that we are observing.

It's easy to think that events, sensations, thoughts and feelings — particularly the ones we don't like — have a hold over us. It's actually the other way around: we have a hold over them. The tension we experience is because we latch on to and pull against what is taking place, but all experiences come and go by themselves if we let them. If we hold on to them then we feel influenced and even dominated by them. That's a great way to feel out of control. It's a paradox, but control naturally restores itself when we let go of attachment and the need to control. It can be very easy to confuse letting go with 'getting rid of', so it might be helpful to consider that when difficult thoughts and emotions arise in the mind, we can simply let them be there, without following them or pushing them away, and simply return our attention to where it needs to be.

Being bound by our experiences is an unconscious habit, not a necessity. We become so habituated to tension that we have come to believe that tension is inevitable and our natural state. But we were not born anxious, preoccupied and distracted; this is a habit we cultivate as we grow up.

Practical examples will help illustrate what's meant by 'holding on' and 'letting go'. Consider, for example, an idea such as, 'I'm no good at maths'. If a student identifies themselves with this idea and can't let it go, it will influence how they feel and behave when confronted by mathematics in the classroom or at home. They will find it hard to engage their attention with the activity of solving the mathematical problem or the teacher's guidance because it is fixated on the idea, 'I'm no good at this, I wish I wasn't here'.

We don't tend to say that we *consider* an opinion but rather that we *hold* an opinion. If we hold on to it then we are much more likely to feel threatened if it's challenged, or deflated if it's proved wrong. This is fertile ground for conflict and loss of objectivity. We often hold onto desires whether they're useful or not. For example, we might cling to a fixed plan such as there only being one course or career that could make us happy. That's a great catalyst for anxiety and fear about results as well as a limitation of creativity and inquiry.

Some assume that letting go is about being passive or not responding even when a response is called for, but mindfulness helps us engage with and respond to events by first letting go of the tension and resistance that often gets in the way of that response. Some think that letting go is about giving all our possessions away but it's essentially giving away our attachment to them. Some think of letting go as 'getting rid of' what we don't like, for example, 'If I let go of a depressive feeling then it will go away'. When we let go of an attachment to an object or emotion we don't feel so fussed by its presence or absence, helping us to cultivate equanimity even in the face of things we find difficult.

Acceptance

Whatever is happening is happening. There's no denying that. At one moment there is comfort, peace, success or happiness. Enjoy it, but remember that it will change so don't get too attached to it. Equally, if there is an experience of pain, anxiety, failure or even depression, then so be it. Be patient — that too will change. Life constantly teaches us that experiences — both pleasurable and painful — come and go whether we like it or not. Dealing with emotional discomfort is an example. If a depressing or worrying thought or feeling comes to our awareness, we might have noticed that the non-acceptance of it — even hating ourselves for feeling it in the first place — leads to a cycle of rumination that merely imprisons our attention on that thought.

Conversely, with acceptance and non-reactivity comes a growing ability to let experiences, whether physical, mental or emotional, flow in and out of our awareness. We can experience them vividly but still be less moved by them. One university student with a long history of depression remarked, 'I thought that because I had a depressing thought I had to think it. Now I realise I don't have to do anything about it, in fact the less I do the easier it is.' That's a very liberating thing. Equally, coming to acceptance of a poor result on a test or assignment will help a student to move on, rather than waste time, by focusing attention on how to improve.

Accepting or being at peace with things isn't easy. It takes time, patience and a fair dose of courage. True acceptance isn't about trying to make something go away, as in, 'If I accept this then it will go away'. That's a good way to get dispirited when the problem, the thing, doesn't go away. Using acceptance to make something go away is actually non-acceptance masquerading as acceptance in order to get rid of that towards which you have a negative attitude. Rather than getting dispirited we would be better to notice what happens when we fight with a situation or experience. It escalates! We could then wonder what would happen if we stopped fighting with it. Through true acceptance, the impact of such experiences starts to diminish and in their own time these experiences impact us less often. It's as if we've been visited by a stray dog that keeps coming back because we keep feeding it, but soon it loses interest and goes away when it is not being fed. Attention is the food that keeps it coming back.

Acceptance is sometimes confused with resignation, giving up and letting things dominate us. At times, we might accept what is happening and allow it to run its course, but at other times we might accept what is happening but also accept what it takes to change it, for instance the effort required to change an unhelpful habit such as procrastination. The well known *Serenity Prayer* by Reinhold Niebuhr is about exactly this:

> ...*[may I have] the serenity to accept the things I cannot change; courage to change the things I can; and wisdom to know the difference.*

Present moment

The present moment is the only moment that has any legitimate claim to reality. The past and future are just ideas. The past and future never actually exist, although in the present we may notice that the mind projects what it imagines the future to be or what it thinks the past was. The residual effects from past thoughts, feelings, actions and decisions may be with us now, but those effects are also only ever observable and experienced in the present moment.

For example, we can feel apprehensive about a class or public speaking engagement coming up the next day. 'Will it go well or will it go badly? What happens if the data projector doesn't work?' ... The night before we might even be standing at the sink washing the dishes thinking, 'I hope I'm in the present moment tomorrow.' How ridiculous hoping to be present while we are practising absent-mindedness. Better to remember, 'If I want to have a chance of being present tomorrow I ought to practise being present now, which means paying attention to these dishes right in front of me!'

We associate 'presence of mind' with being focused, responsive, brave, calm and capable. If we investigate what's going on in the mind when we experience anxiety, fear, depression or worry we will notice that this involves the mind unconsciously slipping into an imaginary future that hasn't happened or reliving a past which has already come and gone. Unfortunately, our focus then slips from what's happening here and now so we don't enjoy the present moment and our experience of it is clouded. When we take this imaginary world to be the real world, the real world doesn't get a look in. When the attention is on the here and now, thoughts of the past or future aren't in the picture and therefore don't cause the emotional upset that they often do. 'Absent-mindedness', of course, is the *opposite* of 'presence of mind'.

In our imaginary future we often catastrophise; that is, imagine problems which never happen. As Mark Twain said, 'I've had a lot of catastrophes in my life, and some of them actually happened'. We concoct anxiety and fear, dwell on rigid ideas about how future events must turn out, and prejudge situations and conversations long before they happen. We become anxious about getting things to go the way we assume they must go, and then experience frustration or grief because they don't go according to those pre-conceived ideas. We prejudice events, which simply means that we judge them before they happen.

After a few weeks of practising mindfulness we may realise that being present is the exception rather than the rule. As shocking as this may be initially, making this realisation is not a matter for concern — it's a sign of increased awareness and therefore progress!

What about planning and preparation? These are vital to functioning in the world. Sometimes people learning mindfulness think that they must never again think of the past or future, but this is a misunderstanding of what mindfulness is. Planning and preparation can be present-moment activities. If we plan or prepare mindfully then it's useful and we do it with intention and attention. Worry, on the other hand, commonly justifies itself by masquerading as preparation. For instance, a student might be so preoccupied about a future exam that they find it hard to focus on the study required to prepare for it. We can be so anxious about the outcome of an interview that we go in tense and unfocused. We can be so preoccupied about the amount of work we have to do that we feel exhausted before having started. Ironically, thinking about work generally consumes more energy than doing it.

Being in the 'here and now' is sometimes associated with being a hedonist who doesn't care about the results of their actions, doesn't care about the future and has no plans or goals. That's not mindfulness. Being present we may enjoy the pleasurable things in life more, but it also means that we know better when to put those things down, when to pick up work, and understand that useful future results are the product of conscious work done in the present. Having a calling, intuition and vision for the future are all highly mindful states. When we're not present we are often fooling ourselves or not noticing the thoughts and feelings really motivating our actions, and the consequences they will bring. The question is, are we going to keep living under the tyranny of our imaginings about the past or future, or are we going to live the life we are meant to be living, here and now, moment by moment, one step at a time?

CHAPTER 2

The science of mindfulness

We've explored some of the philosophy and principles of mindfulness and its relevance to education. But it is also important that we understand a bit of the science and research on mindfulness because this will help us to have more confidence and conviction about the importance of applying and practising mindfulness.

Neuroplasticity

One of the most important findings in the past twenty or so years regarding our understanding of the brain has been the fact that our brain constantly changes in response to what it experiences.[1] It continually produces new connections and pathways between its nearly 100 billion nerve cells (neurons), and can actually sprout new neurons in certain areas of the brain. We used to think the brain largely formed while we were in the womb and, during the first few years of life, went through a few critical periods of refinement where connections we weren't using were pruned back and then the brain remained relatively fixed for the remainder of our life, with slow degeneration as we aged. However, research shows that how we use our brains — and particularly what we pay attention to and practise repeatedly — actually gets hardwired into the brain. We know this because of all the modern brain imaging technology, such as the electroencephalogram (EEG) and functional magnetic resonance imaging (fMRI), that we now have to study how the brain is structured and how it functions. For instance, as people practise the piano, parts of the brain associated with touch sensitivity, fine finger movements and the ability to discriminate between different musical tones become active. And when pianists practise over a sustained period, these brain areas actually *grow*, as neurons form new connections (there are an average of 100 trillion in the brain) and so the neurons move further apart. In many ways the brain can be thought of as a muscle that becomes stronger and more capable as it is used. What is even more fascinating is the fact that *mental* rehearsal (imagining oneself doing an activity without physically doing it) produces the exact same changes. For example, a fascinating study found that a group of people who mentally practised piano scales over a period of just five days (that is, merely thought about playing them without actually touching a piano) showed the exact same changes in their brain as a group of people who did actual practise. [2]

Default mode

But it's not only *what* we pay attention to that matters: *how* we pay attention is also critical. Studies show that when we are not paying attention to something, the brain clicks over into what we now call 'default mode'. You are probably quite familiar with this mode, characterised by inattention, judgment, criticism, mind-wandering and doing things on autopilot rather than experiencing things as they actually are. This impairs our ability to appraise accurately, think clearly, concentrate and learn. And at its extreme, this default mental activity has been associated with a number of mental health problems such as anxiety, depression, attention deficit hyperactivity disorder (ADHD), Alzheimer's disease and even schizophrenia and autism. [3,4,5,6,7,8]

This habit is so ingrained in most of us that we are not even aware it is taking place. It is like the proverbial water that we are swimming in — the very mental environment in which we function. When people start practising mindfulness, one of the first things they notice is how much time they spend in default mode, operating on automatic. They are often quite shocked to discover that their attention tends to be in the present for brief periods in between long periods of daydreaming, mental chatter, worrying about the future or dwelling on the past.

However, in this very act of observing this tendency something remarkable starts to take place. Simply starting to notice what our attention is on immediately begins to change the habit of inattention. Our mind starts to focus on what is actually happening, gets less and less caught up in projections and judgments and reactivity, and recognises faster when it is. The use-it-or-lose-it nature of neuroplasticity actually starts working for, rather than against, us. We start using the parts of the brain that prioritise and direct the attention and they start to work a whole lot better. In fact, simply by training our attention to be in the present, the default mode of the brain starts to become less prevalent. The parts of the brain associated with worrying, dwelling, catastrophising and judging become less active, and the pathways associated with them actually start to be pruned back. Simultaneously, areas of the brain associated with paying attention, learning, memory and psychological wellbeing become activated and start forming new connections and growing new cells. We start to become the conscious architects of our own brains.

Executive function

One of the key areas of the brain associated with the capacity to pay attention is the prefrontal cortex (PFC). The cortex is the surface of the brain, and prefrontal refers to the area just behind the forehead. The PFC is one of the last parts of the brain to form in humans and is also one of the most complex. More than any other part of the brain the PFC distinguishes humans from other animals. It is one of the key brain regions involved in what is called *executive functioning*. This is like the control panel of the brain and involves a number of complex mental processes that regulate things like planning, reasoning, problem solving, focusing and directing attention, short-term (working) memory, mental flexibility, managing emotions (by down-regulating the emotional centre of the brain — the limbic system) and controlling intentional behaviour and inhibiting unwanted behaviours.

The following table outlines the main executive functions and the area of the prefrontal cortex responsible for each.

The prefrontal cortex and key executive functions	
Thinking and reasoning Focusing and directing attention Cognitive flexibility Planning Problem solving Short-term (working) memory	Dorsolateral prefrontal cortex (DLPFC)
Impulse control Self-awareness Understanding emotional states Goal-directed behaviour	Orbitofrontal cortex (OFC)
Controlling intentional behaviour Inhibiting inappropriate behaviour Making decisions	Anterior cingulate cortex (ACC)

One executive function is to imagine the future and recollect the past. This distinctly human ability sets us apart from other animals and is one of the key reasons why humans have been so successful at adapting to — and controlling — the environment. However, if we are unmindful, the ability to project into the future and the past comes at a significant cost because we lose the ability to discern between imagination and reality. When in default mode, we can imagine and remember things that are distressing and reduce our capacity to get a job done just as easily as we can remember things that make us feel good and improve our productivity. Then other parts of the brain, such as the fear centre (amygdala), can hijack our thinking and we can find ourselves locked in a fight or flight stress response.

Mindfulness helps us to discern the reality of the present moment from imagination. The mind can still imagine but at least we see this imagining for what it is, rather than confusing it with reality. Research shows that practising mindfulness activates many of the same brain areas as those that are active when we are engaged in executive functioning. Unsurprisingly then, mindfulness practise has been found to increase many facets of executive functioning, particularly attention, short-term memory, regulating emotional impulses, planning and mental flexibility.[9] Recently a study on tertiary students looked at the effect of brief mindfulness meditation practice on knowledge retention after a class lecture. The post-lecture quiz showed that meditation significantly improved students' retention of the information, which is just another indication of mindfulness improving performance and efficiency of learning.[10] When we are focused, we see the clearest and function the best. We become more able to make discerning choices about what to focus on and what actions to take, or not to take, and become better at consciously *responding* to events rather than habitually *reacting* to them. Once again, these useful changes get hardwired into the brain. So what in the beginning seems to take a lot of effort — i.e. the intentional process of paying attention — gradually becomes effortless and natural. With regular mindfulness practice we start finding ourselves better able to think clearly, regulate our attention and behaviour, and learn and function better in the world.

Multitasking

Learning to focus our attention on one thing at a time increases our productivity. Most people think they can multitask — that is, focus on multiple things at the same time. But it turns out this is a myth. Even for women! Research into what are called 'divided attention' experiments shows that people are able to pay attention to two simple stimuli presented simultaneously, for instance listening to simple sentences through headphones while at the same time pressing a button whenever a blue square pops up on a screen in front of them. But as soon as the stimuli become more complex — for instance reading an email while talking on the phone — or we try to do a number of things at once, we cease dividing our attention and start doing what is called *attention switching*. This is exactly what it sounds like: moving our attention from one thing to another. Like most things, we can get better at this with practice, and it can seem as if we are focusing on many things at the same time, but the reality is that we are never truly holding more than one complex thing in mind at any one time. And there is a serious downside to operating in this way.

What happens when we multitask is that each time we shift our attentional focus from one thing to another, there is a lag time of between 200 and 500 milliseconds (a fifth to a half of a second) where our visual attention is unable to notice anything new. This is called the 'attentional blink'. If we think about this in relation to multitasking, it means that every time we stop focusing on something and check our email or Facebook, we lose up to half a second of focus. Do this enough times during a study session and we can start seriously impairing our productivity and flow. It's like constantly opening apps on a tablet. And research shows that people attempting to multitask are more distracted and disorganised, and have worse analytic reasoning and impaired memory.[11] If we have nothing to compare multitasking to we think there is no other desirable way to be. If we get habituated to it we soon find there is no other way we *can* be. Other research shows that if we stop what we are doing to check an email, it takes over a minute to get our attention fully back to what we were doing. We are starting to talk about some serious inefficiency.

Making this problem even worse, studying in this way actually starts training our executive function to jump our attention around from one thing to another, rather than focusing for sustained periods on what we actually need to focus on. Again, over time, this gets hardwired into the brain and becomes automatic, meaning that we do it without realising — and therefore whether we want to or not. In fact, for most of us, this way of being is already pretty much hardwired. That's why it is called default mode.

Training attention

The good news again is that mindfulness meditation practice can change this habit, but it takes a little time and patience. Intentionally paying attention to a single sensory object — for instance, the feeling of the breath coming and going, or listening to the sounds around you without getting caught up in labelling them or thinking about them — starts to retrain our executive function and we become better able to focus on one thing for longer periods of time. The technical terms for this are self-monitoring and cognitive control. We can then apply this improved focus to anything we like, for instance driving our car, reading, thinking through an issue, teaching or engaging in hobbies.

At the start of this retraining it can be quite difficult to get our focus to remain where we want it. Many people who do our mindfulness courses say early on that it seems as if their mind becomes even *busier* than before they started practising mindfulness. In fact, they sometimes worry that mindfulness is making things worse. What is actually happening is that they are noticing for the first time just how busy the mind is and how scattered their attention is — that is, how little time the mind spends in the present and how often it is jumping around from past to future, from worrying to dwelling to obsessively planning to dwelling and back again. But we can literally 'come to our senses', which refers to the fact that the senses are a gateway back into the present moment. With practice, the participants in our courses are able to start focusing for longer and longer periods on the present, using something they can notice through the senses (e.g. the feeling of their breath coming and going) as an anchor. And, breath by breath, their brain starts to change. A useful metaphor is that of walking through a field of wheat. The first time we walk through we are literally bush bashing — progress is slow and it's hard to find our way. But as we walk the same path over and over again, it gets easier to move through and the path is clearly laid out. Eventually it becomes well trodden and we can move through relatively effortlessly, without having to think about where we are going.

The zone and flow states

Research into states of peak performance or 'flow states', which athletes sometimes refer to as 'being in the zone', shows that these share a strong relationship with mindfulness. Athletes, musicians and dancers, among others, who experience these states describe an experience of intense but effortless focus, where time seems to slow down, thoughts settle and everything becomes calm and clear. It turns out this is a pretty common experience, too. Mihály Csíkszentmihályi, one of the eminent researchers into these states (it's a very difficult name to pronounce so probably better just to call him 'the flow guy'), says that about one in five people report experiencing flow states multiple times throughout the day, during simple activities such as working or playing with their kids. Csíkszentmihályi says that two main things lead to flow states: doing tasks that take us to our limits but are just manageable; and intentionally paying full attention to what we are doing. In the former it happens because we have no reasonable alternative but to be fully present and in the latter we have consciously made the choice to do it. However, while this paying of attention to the just-manageable task can initially be quite effortful, it soon becomes easier and less effortful, and then we just find ourselves in the zone. Some footballers talk about going in and out of the zone multiple times throughout a game, at times needing to deliberately focus on the play and at others just going with the flow, so to speak. At times thoughts enter the mind and these can pull us out of flow states, especially when the thoughts are intense or critical and we react to them. Simply bringing a non-judgmental awareness to such thoughts, letting them go by without reacting to them and redirecting our attention to the task once again — whether it be a football game, piano concerto or simply doing maths homework — can get us straight back into flow once again.

Stress, mental health and wellbeing

But mindfulness is not just about brain performance, productivity and flow states. There is a rapidly expanding body of evidence that mindfulness can reduce stress and improve health and wellbeing, too. In fact, mindfulness is now widely used in medicine and healthcare to treat a wide range of psychological issues, from anxiety and depression to ADHD and behavioural problems, addiction, eating and sleep issues, personality disturbances, psychosis and more. A review of all existing studies conducted by Stefan Hofmann and his team found that mindfulness was a promising intervention for treating mental health disorders and improving psychological and physical wellbeing.[12] Research has shown that it also helps people manage physical problems such as chronic pain, psoriasis and cancer, and can even lead to a slowing of the ageing process down to the level of our DNA.[13]

One of the reasons that mindfulness is so effective for these issues is that paying attention to the present moment without reacting to what is happening is the opposite process to those that underpin stress, anxiety and depression. If we start paying attention to the process, we will invariably start to notice that when we are stressed our mind will be either in the past, dwelling on something that didn't go so well and thinking of all the ways we would like to change it, or worrying about some negative future event that may never even happen. This habit is pervasive — just watch your own mind for a day, or even just the next 60 seconds!

And when our mind is off somewhere else, generally imagining the worst or remembering things that didn't go well for us, this actually triggers a sympathetic nervous response. The sympathetic nervous system is the part of our central nervous system that prepares the body for action: it wakes us up in the morning, increases our alertness when something seems important or dangerous, and dumps adrenaline to increase our heart rate when we have to move quickly. It is responsible for the fight or flight response. This is a useful response to have when we nearly step on a snake and have to get out of the way (or look up to see a bus suddenly coming right at us) but it is more of a liability when the 'snake' is actually a rope: that is, something such as an exam or deadline that is not inherently life-threatening but that we misperceive as such and react to accordingly with a stress response.

In the grip of a stress response we experience increased heart rate, thickening of the blood, and movement of the blood away from the gut and the skin and toward the large muscles in the legs and arms, ready to run or fight. Digestion stops and blood sugar and fat levels rise (fuel to burn) and we start breathing fast to get oxygen on board in order to burn the fuel. On a brain level we have difficulty moving our attention away from the threat, so that it is amplified and looms large in our mind, soon occupying all of our attention. If we are anxious rather than focused, the parts of the brain associated with reasoning and judgment switch off in favour of other more primitive brain areas such as the limbic system (the 'emotional brain' mentioned previously, that regulates and influences responses to emotions, mood and memory) and the even deeper structures commonly referred to as the reptilian brain. And so, in situations where we are unmindful and we misperceive ropes as imaginary snakes, it can literally become 'snake on snake' as we revert to ancient — generally unhelpful and even destructive — behavioural patterns to confront the situation. These patterns include becoming angry and aggressive, avoiding things we need to address or numbing out with drugs and alcohol. When the sympathetic nervous system gets so activated that it becomes overloaded it can even short out, producing a freeze response, such as when a rabbit suddenly sees an eagle overhead, tenses up completely and ceases all movement. In humans, this tends to show up more as procrastination and the inability to get started on tasks that need doing.

Left unchecked, over the longer term the stress response can impair biological functions such as appetite and sleep, create imbalances in the body leading to physical illness, accelerate ageing and can also produce mental disturbance and behavioural problems. This is sometimes called 'high allostatic load' and creates wear and tear on the body. It can lead to addictions as we try maladaptively to reduce arousal or relax through the use of substances, television, food and so on.

Mindfulness, of course, offers an alternative to this. It allows us to simply notice with ever greater clarity when our mind is off somewhere else, particularly when this is causing us stress, and return it to the present moment, back to what *is* rather than 'what if'. Teaching mindfulness meditation to people with mental health problems has been shown to reduce symptoms and improve wellbeing and quality of life. It has also been linked with improved resilience. Furthermore, in research we have done we have found that people who are naturally more mindful recover from depression and anxiety disorders faster than people who are less intrinsically mindful.[14] Even people who do not have clinical depression or anxiety experience improvements in wellbeing and mood.

Mindfulness turns out to also be very effective for dealing with physical as well as emotional pain. The ability to redirect the attention to what you are doing, rather than being lost in reacting to pain and discomfort, is very helpful. In addition, the acceptance aspect of mindfulness is a very useful antidote to the usual patterns of reactivity and resistance that people have to physical illness and pain. Jon Kabat-Zinn, one of the pioneers of the use of mindfulness in medicine and healthcare, began by using mindfulness with intractable chronic pain patients. These were people with illnesses and injuries that caused at times incapacitating pain, and for whom standard medical treatments such as surgery, medication, therapy and hypnosis had been unsuccessful. Kabat-Zinn observed a pattern in all of these unsuccessful treatments: they were all attempts to get *away* from the pain and discomfort. Kabat-Zinn had spent long periods of time meditating and had experienced first-hand the ability to systematically change the relationship to one's own discomfort by observing it objectively and not taking it so personally — having it be simply *pain* as an objective sensation rather than 'my' pain. In a sense it is about changing the reference point from being immersed in the pain to being an impartial observer of it. He adapted some meditations he had practised into simple but effective practices that proved highly successful at helping around 80 per cent of his patients change their relationship with their chronic pain in exactly this way. They were then able to 'have their pain rather than it having them', and were able to get on with their lives. It makes you think Shakespeare may have been a closet mindfulness practitioner when he said, 'nothing is either good or bad but thinking makes it so'. Actually, Kabat-Zinn's program was so successful that it quickly expanded and moved out of the hospital basement into its own dedicated area, and eventually began being used by different hospitals and treatment centres. People also started reporting that practising these very same exercises reduced their levels of stress, anxiety and depression, and so mindfulness began being used more widely in psychology and psychiatry.

Mindfulness is also, for obvious reasons, a very effective antidote for attentional problems such as ADHD. If we consider that we all have a mild form of ADHD, particularly when we constantly live in a time-pressured environment or multitask and jump from one thing to the next, it becomes clear how systematically training the attention is useful for people who have more trouble than most focusing. That tends to deal with the 'AD' part. As for the 'H' in ADHD — the hyperactivity — mindfulness offers the ability to sit with discomfort and to 'urge surf'. This term, coined by Alan Marlatt, refers to being able to observe urges — for instance, to scratch an itch or check Facebook when you are trying to work — without reacting to them or being controlled by them. We can notice how they increase and peak and then eventually fade away, all by themselves, the less we keep reactivating them. This decreased reactivity allows people with ADHD to have greater control over their behaviours and reactions. This same capacity is also extremely helpful for people with addictions, where the ability to surf urges rather than giving in to them is obviously central to recovery. Accordingly, mindfulness is being used more and more to treat addictions, whether to drugs, cigarettes and alcohol, television, the internet, pornography, or food.

In a similar way, mindfulness can help with behavioural problems. The mental space that comes with mindfulness practice — that is, the ability to see thoughts as just mental phenomena rather than facts, and to observe them rather than react to them — allows people to be less impulsive and driven by attempts to avoid discomfort. Mindfulness is even effective in dealing with extreme behavioural issues such as self-harm and suicidal behaviours in people with personality disturbances such as borderline personality disorder.

•

So, to sum up, in this chapter we have seen how the brain changes its connections and actually grows new cells in response to what we experience and practice. This means that something like mindfulness, where we systematically train our attention to remain in the present and be non-reactive, can literally shape our brain in ways that make it much easier to concentrate, remember and learn, regulate emotions and behaviours, reason and think abstractly. Learning to pay attention can improve performance in all areas of our lives, from the sporting field to the classroom, our relationships and our home life. It can even lead to flow states, whereby we function at full capacity yet with almost no effort. Mindfulness can also increase resilience, reduce the effects of stress and psychological issues, and improve wellbeing and quality of life. It is therefore of great potential use in educational settings, where peak brain performance is an asset and where many stress and mental health issues tend to emerge. A number of these issues will be explored in more detail in coming chapters, and suggestions will be made for practical ways to bring mindfulness into the classroom to enhance learning outcomes and help teachers cope better with the increasing demands on them.

CHAPTER 3

Stress, focus and performance

A man by the name of John Biggs described the varying ways in which students approach learning and studying and whether or not this was a good predictor of student performance. He defined the characteristics of student motivation and learning strategies and came up with three learning styles: surface, achieving and deep. Although Biggs didn't discuss the relationship of learning style to mindfulness we have added this to his original outline.

Learning styles[1]			
APPROACH	MOTIVE	STRATEGY	ATTENTION
Surface	The main purpose is to meet the study requirements minimally and to achieve a balance between not working too hard versus failing. The main aim is to avoid failure.	The strategy is to gain the bare essentials and reproduce them through rote learning.	In the absence of interest or engagement, the surface learner is easily distracted and struggles to compel their attention to go to the subject he or she is studying.

APPROACH	MOTIVE	STRATEGY	ATTENTION
Achieving	Based on competition and ego enhancement. The aim is to gain the highest grades, whether or not the material is interesting. Usefulness for profession or life is not of concern, only the marks.	Based on efficiently organising one's time and working, and to behave as a 'model' student.	The achieving learner mostly uses pressure or background stress to direct the attention to the subject of study. Can be efficient but attention can be scattered when stress increases too much.
Deep	Learning motivation is intrinsic. Study is done to satisfy interest and maximise competence in particular academic subjects. This approach is also called mastery in other theories.	Students read widely and relate meaningfully with previous relevant knowledge. There is an interest in the interconnectedness of subjects and their future application.	Deep learners' attention is relatively effortlessly engaged with the subject being studied because it is naturally drawn by the positive motivation of interest.

Our learning styles can be a mixture of these three or vary from one subject to another. For example, we might be a deep learner for a topic we are interested in — whether it's a school subject such as biology or our favourite hobby or sport — and a surface learner for the things we aren't interested in. The good thing is that deep learners' learning is mostly driven by interest, engagement and enjoyment rather than stress and is therefore relatively effortless compared to other learning styles. Interest is a magnet for attention, and where interest goes enjoyment follows. Deep learners also have the most flexible and creative minds because they are most engaged with the content for its own sake rather than for the sake of something else, such as avoiding failure or enhancing one's self-esteem by getting a good mark. The paradox is that despite less stress, deep learners also do the best. Studies on university students suggest that First or Second Class Honours students all used deep approaches whereas Third Class Honours students tended to use surface approaches.[2]

There is a positive correlation between anxiety and performance on exams for students whose motivation was achievement or failure avoidance (surface) and to that extent one can say that stress is a good thing for performance. Students who are deep learners don't *have to be* anxious to do well. It's not that they never feel pressure but just that it is far less predominant and they have a positive motivation (such as enjoyment, commitment, fascination) rather than a negative one (e.g. fear, anxiety, avoidance of embarrassment). The temptation to cheat or plagiarise is also related to learning approach, with deep learners the least likely to do it compared to achievement and surface learners.

Teaching styles

Although Biggs never looked at teaching styles, there are good questions for a teacher to ask themselves such as, 'What motivates my teaching?', 'What strategies am I going to foster in my students?' or 'Am I really interested in the topic myself?'. A teacher who is a 'surface teacher' (just doing the minimum to satisfy requirements) or an 'achievement teacher' (primarily driven by anxiety about students getting high marks) is likely to bring out these attitudes in their students. We might be thinking we're teaching students about a subject but, without us or them really knowing it, we might be teaching them far more about how to, or how not to, learn. It's not that marks are not important, but a teacher who loves their subject and is driven by interest will engage their own attention and that of their students in an entirely different and more authentic way. Such teachers inspire their students and really help them to achieve at the same time, and these passionate and enthusiastic teachers are the ones you remember all your life.

The relationship between stress and performance

It's very common that students use stress and only stress to motivate themselves and drive performance. Hence, many are reluctant to reduce stress, fearing that this will undermine productivity because of the assumption that there are only two states — apathy or stress. If we associate being 'relaxed' with being unmindful and unmotivated then we think, 'How can I afford to relax? I wouldn't get anything done.' Over time, as stress becomes habituated, we think that this is normal and there is no other alternative. Whether it's the pressure of getting an assignment submitted on time or a looming exam, pretty soon we can't even fling off the bedclothes in the morning without some kind of pressure to make us do it.

The relationship between stress and performance is summarised by Yerkes and Dodson in the 'stress–performance curve' (Diagram 1). It illustrates how inertia, apathy, procrastination or boredom are low stress states. There's no stress but there's also no performance: 'I've got all the time in the world to prepare for the exam. I think I'll spend another few hours surfing the net.' This is generally a time when parents and teachers get anxious about the lack of progress and are anything but reassured by the students' assurances that 'It's all under control'. Closer to the exam or assignment deadline anxiety builds and denial doesn't work like it used to, and eventually performance improves but time is short now. If the stress is not too high or prolonged then all is relatively well. If we are really lucky then we are at the top of the stress–performance curve and we tolerate the temporary increase in pressure and are able to maintain performance, albeit at a price.

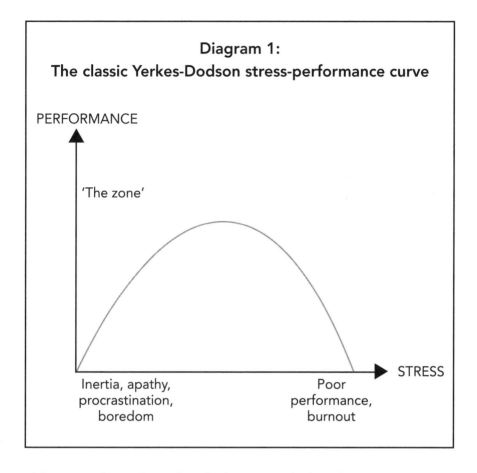

Diagram 1:
The classic Yerkes-Dodson stress-performance curve

PERFORMANCE

'The zone'

STRESS

Inertia, apathy,
procrastination,
boredom

Poor
performance,
burnout

If, however, demands escalate further or we find we have more to cover than we thought, or if something goes wrong such as illness, then we fall behind and the stress goes up further. Having conditioned ourselves to drive performance only with stress, we naturally push harder. We might even pull a few all-nighters, get behind in sleep, and soon feel terrible and find it hard to maintain the level of effort required. We also start to lose our focus. Now we really begin to run into problems as the stress escalates but performance drops off rather than improves. This is a 'lose–lose' situation where despite higher stress our performance decreases rather than goes to a higher level. We have 'gone over the top' and if it goes on for too long then we are prime candidates for burnout. This problem is generally compounded by being unorganised, prioritising poorly and multitasking, all of which simply amplify stress and reduce efficiency.

There is another possibility when demands are high, as illustrated by the Hassed 'mindfulness-based stress-performance curve' (Diagram 2).[3] If we reflect for a moment on those times when we were functioning at our peak we may notice that it feels unusual in a number of ways. As discussed earlier, athletes and creative artists talk about being in 'the zone' or a 'flow state' and students often experience the same state while studying at their best or even during exams. In this state there is no stress; in fact it is quite the opposite. We feel calm, enlivened, confident, in touch, insightful, responsive, efficient and energised. This is by far the most enjoyable and sustainable level of performance. Although the outer circumstances might appear to be pressured, the inner state is one of calmness and clarity, and attention is entirely in the moment on the process and not preoccupied about the potential outcome. This is our most mindful state and confounds usual assumptions about what it takes to perform at a high level. Why? Increasing mindfulness has two significant effects. First, because attention is less drawn to anxieties, fears, rumination and concerns, there is a reduction in stress and a feeling of inner calmness. Second, focus on task means we are alert and responsive to what is in front of us. Paradoxically, we cannot think our way into the zone, but through mindfulness we can practise not thinking our way out of it.

Just to illustrate the point, a study showed that teachers receiving a Mindfulness-Based Stress Reduction program experienced significant reductions in psychological symptoms and burnout, and improvements in observer-rated classroom organisation, performance on a computer task of affective attentional bias (i.e. negative moods did not disrupt their focus), and an increase in self-compassion (i.e. they were kinder to themselves). The control group showed measures of worsening stress and burnout levels. The more the teachers enhanced their mindfulness the better were the outcomes in terms of psychological symptoms, burnout and sustained attention.[4]

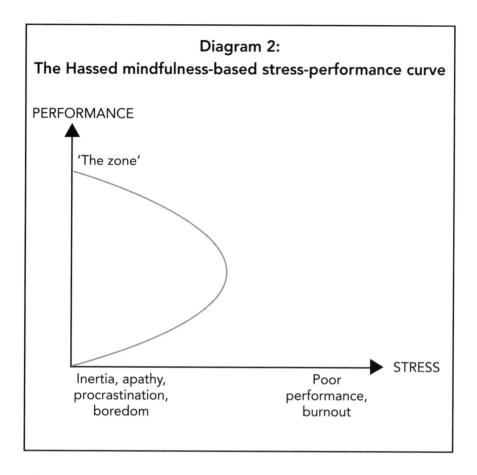

Diagram 2:
The Hassed mindfulness-based stress-performance curve

PERFORMANCE

'The zone'

STRESS

Inertia, apathy,
procrastination,
boredom

Poor
performance,
burnout

There is an important distinction to be made between stress and the alertness associated with being mindful. High stress is associated with poorer executive functioning and hence poor performance, whereas being mindful is associated with better executive functioning and better performance as discussed in the last chapter. An overactive stress centre in the brain (amygdala) hijacks executive functioning, making functioning effectively difficult if not impossible. Working or short-term memory is our immediate memory of what's happening currently and we rely on it to learn, create and perform complex tasks. Aside from attention regulation it's our most important executive function.[5] ADHD is associated with impairment of the areas of the brain associated with executive functioning but even for people without ADHD we perform and learn poorly when under stress. A reduced working-memory capacity leads to a pronounced increase in reaction time and errors and is associated with poor performance in exams.[6,7] It's little wonder what effect it has on a well-intentioned child trying to perform under the gaze of a well-intentioned adult, at home or in the classroom, putting pressure on the child to get the right results.

Taking the time to settle and focus before engaging in an activity, whether it be studying, doing an assignment or preparing for an exam, is not something that most people tend to do, nor is it something that the world at large recognises as being a valuable use of time. But it is!

CHAPTER 4

Why attention matters

The cost of unmindfulness

There are two main forms of resistance to integrating mindfulness in our lives. Firstly, the resistance that comes with having no interest in mindfulness at all; for example, believing that it's a total waste of time, it's nothing more than sitting around doing a whole lot of nothing, it's just contemplating your navel, or it's just a case of being self-indulgent and preoccupied with yourself. This is not an entirely uncommon attitude, at least initially, and it indicates a lack of insight and experience.

Secondly, the resistance experienced by people who have heard about mindfulness, have had a taste of it, and are even interested to integrate it into their lives. Those good intentions very quickly get undermined with an opposing force along the lines of apathy, being too busy to stop, experiencing difficulties in the practice, or forever putting it off until later.

The first form of resistance can be addressed with information, an actual taste of experience, or hearing the testimony of peers who have benefited from mindfulness. The person may even have an appreciation of the importance of being focused or engaged in day-to-day life, but just hadn't used the word mindfulness to describe it. The second form of resistance needs guidance, encouragement and, if possible, the support of a group. To foster motivation, both can benefit from reflecting on the cost of being unmindful.

To think that mindfulness is unnecessary or irrelevant is a little like thinking that light is unnecessary or irrelevant — as if we could get along fine without it. But if there is no light, if we're going about in the dark, then we can't see and understand things, we can't do things, we have accidents and life can get a little scary. Well, it's a bit the same with being unmindful. What we don't pay attention to is in the dark — unseen, unconscious, unacknowledged, unappreciated and misunderstood. Being unaware is not a good recipe for being happy, nor does it help in learning or functioning well. From a mindfulness perspective, ignorance is definitely not bliss. Conversely, what we pay attention to will be 'illuminated' by our awareness. This can be confronting at first, as we possibly begin to notice the previously unnoticed mess of judgments and reactions in our minds. But as we start to see more clearly the piles of rubbish, potholes and sharp objects, we can start to neaten them up, throw them out, put them in order or avoid dangerous obstacles.

What is the cost?

Let's explore practical examples from an education and learning perspective and see whether unmindfulness really works. The list below is not a comprehensive one but describes a few of the important issues participants offer when asked the question, 'What is the cost of unmindfulness in your life?' No doubt, if you stop and reflect for a while, you could add a few more of your own.

Wasting time

For example, we might have to read and reread the same thing again and again because our mind keeps wandering off without us realising. We keep going off on tangents and take much longer to do something than if we were really focused. We procrastinate and take ten times as long thinking about a task than it would have taken to actually do it. Being unmindful wastes a huge amount of time. As a rule of thumb, there is always enough time, energy and resources to get things done but only if we use our time, energy and resources in a focused way.

Not understanding things

Consider the number of times we don't understand what someone is trying to explain to us. Are we mindful by listening and looking at what we are being shown or is our attention misdirected to an internal dialogue such as 'I can't do this' or 'They think I'm an idiot' or 'When is this going to be over?'. If we can't pay attention to the things we need to learn then we won't understand them.

Mental roadblocks

When unmindful we don't even see, or can't find our way around, the mental mind-blocks we have. A mind-block, or a fixed mindset such as 'I'm hopeless at this', stops our attention from engaging with the person or issue we need to learn about. If we're not even able to see the block then we can't make a conscious decision about whether that's what we want to be ruled by.

Poor emotional wellbeing

We often wonder where our fear, frustration, depression and anxiety come from. What causes them? Why do they keep dogging us? Why can't we be free of them? Why do they impact so much on our lives, especially at times when we want them the least, such as during exam time? Well, we may never have stopped for long enough to see what is going on behind the scenes, the kinds of thoughts we are feeding our attention on, our reactions and attitudes to our emotional state, and the effects that those reactions and attitudes have.

Not enjoying life

We don't enjoy something if we are not really there when it happens. We go through the motions of eating our food, having a conversation, listening to music or going for a walk, but the experience is superficial and far less vivid if we are not really connected to it at the time. Anhedonia (a lack of pleasure or enjoyment) is one of the key symptoms of depression because when depressed we tend to be least mindful and engaged with life.

Can't sleep

When unmindful, especially in the middle of the night, the mind is going over reruns of what happened the day before, what might or might not happen tomorrow or at the end of the year, or the what ifs and maybes about progress at school or university.

Communicating poorly

We only listen superficially, or not at all, when we don't really pay attention during conversations. At the very least it means we miss details, but it also affects the quality and depth of our interactions. Communicating while multitasking has not made this any easier.

More distractible

If we practise distraction we get good at it. We may not think much about it initially, but over time we increasingly find that even when we really want to engage with something, such as focusing on revising for an exam or writing an assignment, we find that the mind keeps running off and resisting getting on with the work. It is very frustrating and wasteful.

Lack of motivation

The things that we enjoy are easiest to keep our attention on, but some things are important or necessary to attend to even though the mind is not so interested. Though we procrastinate, avoid, wrestle with ourselves, curse and walk around the block and lie awake at night, we find it hard to get motivated. Conversely, one of the hallmarks of successful and happy people is that they can get on with the things that are necessary even when another aspect of themselves would rather not.

Poor memory

If we don't pay attention to something then, in a sense, we didn't really notice it happen even if it happened right in front of our eyes. If we don't notice it in the first place, we cannot remember it — or at least not well — because it didn't have a chance to register. Compare that with the most vivid and rich experiences in our lives: we remember them really well because we are most mindful when we experience them.

Effects on the brain

It may or may not be apparent to us, but unmindfulness slowly but steadily affects the brain. If you're not paying attention the brain doesn't get the stimulation and exercise it needs, so it doesn't develop connections effectively when young and it ages faster as an adult. The brain needs connection, awareness and engagement: mindfulness.

•

When we total it all up, being unmindful costs us a lot more than we might have realised and so the case for cultivating mindfulness becomes a 'no brainer'. The only way that we can continue to think that mindfulness is not for us is to continue in a state of denial. Once we get over denial then the challenge is how to get over the habitual resistance to cultivating it.

It doesn't really matter what word we want to use for it. Mindfulness is for everyone. Whether we want to practise mindfulness meditation, practise mindfulness informally in our day-to-day lives or cultivate a more mindful attitude to life, we all need awareness. There is nothing useful, enjoyable and fulfilling about living in the dark.

CHAPTER 5
Applied mindfulness

So far we have explored what mindfulness is and how it can help us to learn more effectively. We have also seen how there is a lot of research now demonstrating the benefits of mindfulness for managing stress, increasing resilience and wellbeing and improving our ability to learn. In this chapter we will outline in general terms how mindfulness can be applied to educational settings to improve learning outcomes. In later chapters we will go into more detail and outline specific applications for mindfulness, such as improving cognitive performance, increasing mental flexibility and creativity, reducing stress, fostering emotional development, improving communication and relationships, and navigating the challenges posed by the rapidly increasing use of technology and social media. This chapter is not about the clinical applications of mindfulness. For that, we would refer readers to *Mindfulness for Life*, co-authored by one of the authors of this book, Craig Hassed.

Ultimately, all mindfulness is applied mindfulness. The programs that we run all teach mindfulness in its generic sense but also have a specific goal or intention. Generally this includes things like stress reduction and performance enhancement. It is possible to teach mindfulness without an explicit focus — just teaching people to be more mindfully aware simply for the sake of being more aware. But for many people when there are no clear goals for applying mindfulness, it actually makes it very hard to grasp it. We have found that the more explicit the focus is in our programs, the more easily people grasp what mindfulness is. They then tend to go on to generalise mindfulness to other areas of their lives, sometimes in quite unexpected ways. For instance, participants in our programs often begin by learning how to study more effectively but then find that they also begin communicating more mindfully with loved ones, benefitting their relationships. One young woman did a mindful eating exercise (a commonly used mindfulness practice which involves eating a single sultana but taking 5 minutes to do so) and then realised that, as she put it, 'life is just a series of sultanas, one after another', clearly demonstrating that she had fully grasped the meaning of moment-to-moment awareness through that exercise. The penny really dropped for her. Having a specific focus facilitates learning mindfulness just as having a sport or exercise class helps focus our efforts to improve our fitness in a way that just 'trying to be fitter' tends not to.

It may therefore be useful to talk about *applied mindfulness* and to set this apart conceptually from mindfulness simply as a way of being. Applied mindfulness refers to doing things with the intention of being fully present while doing them. When we do that, we also learn a lot about how our mind and body work, so there's a lot of practical value that follows on from being present. In fact, at Monash University where we both work, we have designed a number of mindfulness programs with exactly this in mind. The remainder of this chapter will explore in detail one of these programs, Mindfulness for Academic Success (MAS), to help illustrate what applied mindfulness can look like. Although the program was originally developed for university students, we regularly adapt it for students of any age.

Mindfulness is proven to help stress, anxiety and depression, and is being used more and more widely in educational contexts, both in individual counselling and in preventative and resilience-building programs. Many programs, however, teach students mindfulness and then leave them to figure out on their own how to apply it to their studies. Some of these applications are obvious — for instance, learning to focus on the present has an immediate, universal benefit for studying. Being able to let go of negative and critical thoughts about one's performance likewise aids performance and protects against anxiety and depression. And as we have said, these benefits tend to generalise to things such as relationships and self-care.

MAS is an innovative program where students are taught specifically how to apply mindfulness to their study. Basic mindfulness practices are taught, such as the body scan and mindfulness of breathing. These core practices develop the ability to be present and alert, learning to redirect the attention to the five senses whenever it wanders off, while letting go of judgment and self-criticism. These principles and practices are then applied directly to managing stress (this will be explored in detail in Chapter 17) and improving study performance by learning to sustain attention and focus over a period of time, developing presence of mind rather than trying to multitask (which is highly inefficient, as we saw in Chapter 2), and overcoming procrastination.

The two core mindfulness practices can be found in Chapter 20: Exercise 1, 'Body scan' (p. 200) and Exercise 2, 'Using the breath as an anchor' (p. 205).

To illustrate how this works, let's explore one of the MAS sessions in detail. Session three is titled 'Choosing to stay focused'. We give it this name to emphasise the intentional nature of redirecting the attention back to the present any time we notice we have gone off into default mode. As outlined earlier in the book, with just the smallest amount of mindfulness practice, students can start to observe this tendency and *choose* to simply redirect their attention back to the class or their study. Session three teaches students to make this choice more consciously and wisely, over and over and over again, until they strengthen their executive functioning and become more effective at studying.

Session three introduces a mindfulness meditation called 'thought labelling'. It develops the ability to recognise the actual content of their thoughts. Students are instructed to focus their attention on their breathing, noticing any time their mind wanders off, and simply bringing it back without resisting or following the thoughts or distractions. Then, after they have done that for a short time, they are instructed to observe *what* distracts them from moment to moment. They are offered a number of *categories* of potential distractions, such as 'daydreaming', 'planning', 'judging', 'criticising', 'remembering', 'worrying', 'feeling' (body sensations such as hunger), and 'listening' (to sounds around them). These categories help them to start noticing more clearly the kinds of things that distract them when they are trying to pay attention to something (in this case, their breathing). And they soon realise that it is these very same things that tend to hijack them when they are trying to study.

Mindfulness meditation, used in this way, is akin to a scientific laboratory. We reduce the number of irrelevant things and simplify the environment as much as possible — for instance, by closing our eyes and choosing to focus on a single thing, in this case the breath. And then we can start to observe with much greater clarity what is actually happening in our minds from moment to moment.

This exercise is then extended further to show participants explicitly how to apply these principles to their studies. They are given a written exercise — in the MAS program they get a choice between a 'spot-the-difference' game, a Sudoku or a reading comprehension task. Of course, participants are instructed to notice *why* they chose the task they did, since every moment in a mindfulness program can be used to increase awareness.

Participants are then instructed to direct their full focus to this written task, just as they had previously been directing their focus to their breath. So in a very real sense this exercise becomes a 'study meditation' or a 'problem-solving meditation'. The written task, we should add, occupies the left-hand column of a landscape-oriented A4 sheet. The right half of the sheet is blank. As participants begin working on the task, they are instructed to observe any time their attention wanders off and make a mark in the right-hand column of the sheet, then to let it go and return their attention to the task. If they notice what it is that hijacks their attention — the actual thought, reaction or environmental distracter — they are instructed to write it down then redirect their attention once more to the task.

Fully acknowledging and accepting distractions — in this case by writing them down — actually helps to more easily and fully let go of them. Often the students notice themselves remembering bills that need to be paid or something they had temporarily forgotten that is important to remember. Trying to simply let these go tends not to work — at best, the thought gets parked in short-term memory, just out of view, but pops up every so often just to make sure it doesn't get forgotten! Writing them down on a piece of paper reassures them that they will not be forgotten, and this allows them to be let go of more fully.

After 10 minutes we debrief the exercise in the group. Students generally start to notice that they tend to get distracted by similar things during the written task as when they are attending to their breath. Hearing about the experience of other members of the group also highlights how common distraction is; it can be very useful to realise they are not alone and that this is universal stuff. They also recognise how common certain types of distractions are, such as self-criticism, comparing their performance with others (which tends to reduce confidence and, ultimately, performance), and getting bored. This normalising of difficulties is one of the most important things that comes out of participating in mindfulness courses — students often start the program thinking that everyone else is fine and distraction, self-criticism and procrastination happen only to them, and are often relieved to hear that these things affect everyone (including the group facilitators) in similar ways.

The students are then encouraged to keep a pad next to them while they study at home so they can write down any distractions, let them go, and return their attention to their study. This real-life practice helps them integrate mindfulness more fully into their studying. It also tends to show them more clearly the kinds of distractions and mental tendencies that get in the way of studying effectively.

In session four, the same line of enquiry is extended even further by beginning an exploration of what actually happens when we procrastinate — that is, what thoughts and distractions enter the mind that we then get caught up in rather than getting started on our work? Again, procrastination is normalised and framed as a *habit* — which, by virtue of being viewed in this way, can be changed with a little patient effort. Procrastination, like anything, is something we can 'practise' and get extremely good at — but getting an A+ in procrastination is not likely to look good on an academic transcript.

Linking the mindfulness meditation (in this case, thought labelling) with study in this way helps the students to fully grasp how mindfulness can be used to improve their academic performance. It trains their capacity to focus attention (through directing attention to a single object, whether the breath or a written exercise) and also increases awareness of default-brain tendencies that hijack study and reduce performance. It provides students with an opportunity to engage with mindfulness on a number of levels, both experientially (i.e. the practice of focusing and letting go) and conceptually (recognising what distracts them and beginning to develop strategies to address this), as well as having their difficulties normalised by the group.

As we have already said, participants in mindfulness programs naturally tend to make these links. Indeed, one of the biggest strengths of mindfulness is how it can be applied to so many different things. However, designing applied mindfulness programs such as MAS helps teach students to use mindfulness to effectively target specific challenges that they face, rather than assuming that they will work it out for themselves — which our experience shows happens often but not always.

We hope this chapter has provided you with a clear sense of how generic mindfulness principles and skills may be applied to specific study challenges. You may even like to experiment with the MAS exercise outlined — research we have done on MAS shows that it is extremely effective for improving academic performance and also tends to result in improved emotional wellbeing as people come to rely less on harsh discipline and self-criticism to motivate themselves and increasingly recognise that they can just train their awareness and capacity to notice and let go of distractions.

In the next chapter, we will explore more explicitly how mindfulness practice can be used to improve attentional focus, and the benefits of undertaking this training.

CHAPTER 6

Sharpening the tool

Using mindfulness to improve attention and memory

We hope by now it is clear why learning to pay attention, which involves acknowledging and then letting go of distractions, is useful for learning. In fact, it is vital. Recall William James' statement from Chapter 1 that the ability to pay attention lies at the heart of operating effectively in the world, as well as his lament that there were no effective methods for bringing this about. Some of the ways mindfulness can help address this were outlined in Chapter 2. In this chapter we explore in more detail how attention operates and how mindfulness provides an extremely effective tool for improving this capacity. If students (or anybody) get that working well, a lot of other things become possible, such as improved memory and better overall academic performance.

Training attention

Give me six hours to chop down a tree and I will spend the first four sharpening the axe.

Abraham Lincoln

This statement, from one of the great statesmen of history, speaks to the importance of intentionally training our attention. Students tend to learn this by default throughout their many years at school, sitting and paying attention to what is being taught. But it is largely left up to students to develop this on their own. Mindfulness offers an effective, practical way to intentionally develop the capacity to pay attention. Learning to ground our attention in the present, through the five senses (and, later, through consciously attending to thoughts) improves one's ability to pay attention to what is happening in each moment. When this is systematically trained — either formally, during periods of mindfulness meditation, or informally through the day — changes in the structure of the prefrontal cortex improve executive functioning. This, in turn, allows for better control of attention.

One useful distinction to make here is between two different broad types of meditation — *concentration* and *mindfulness*. This distinction is often overlooked when people talk about mindfulness or meditation and so the two types are often confused. There is substantial overlap between them, but there are also some key differences that have particular implications when applied to the context of education.

Concentration meditation involves focusing the attention on one thing, which is why it is sometimes called 'focused attention' meditation.[1] This may be something happening through the senses, or a sound, word or statement repeated mentally (commonly referred to as a *mantra*). Whatever is focused on in this way is called a 'meditation object'. During concentration meditation, the attention is fixed on the meditation object, and becomes more and more focused. As this focus increases, the attention also becomes increasingly absorbed by the object, and the meditator begins to cease noticing other sensory objects. This can reach a point where the attention is like a laser beam and is focused entirely on the breath. A feeling of wellbeing appears as worries and concerns fade into the background. Transcendental meditation (TM) is a common example of this kind of meditation, although simply focusing on the breath in a single-pointed way achieves the same effect.

In contrast to the laser-like quality of concentration meditation, mindfulness involves having a wider, softer focus. Think of a torch with a beam of light that can be focused on a particular point. Practising mindfulness is more like having the beam expanded wide so that more of what is happening in each moment is noticed, rather than just one single object. As we have already outlined, when practising mindfulness, the attention is often directed to a single object — such as the breath coming and going — but other body sensations, sounds, smells, tastes and thoughts are all allowed to come and go. They are noticed and acknowledged, but without the meditator getting caught up in them.

Each type of meditation can be useful for different purposes. Practising concentration meditation to sharpen attention can be extremely useful for developing the ability to focus. This is useful for everyone, and particularly students with concentration difficulties such as those with ADHD. Training single-pointedness may also come in very handy if you need to focus intensely on a complex maths equation. Mindfulness, in contrast, helps us develop the ability to remain centred and present while at the same being able to attend to other things that are going on around us — if they are relevant. For instance, it would make more sense for students to sit mindfully in class, paying attention to what is being taught, rather than focusing single-pointedly on the breath to the exclusion of everything else.

Brain imaging research shows that each type of meditation activates different brain regions, largely in the prefrontal cortex (which we discussed in Chapter 2).[2] However, it may be more appropriate to think of each as the opposite end of a single dimension, rather than two distinct types of meditation.[3] Different examples of each type of meditation are listed in the following table.

Common examples of mindfulness and concentration meditation	
ACTIVITY	TYPE
Body scan	Mindfulness
Mindfulness of breathing	Mindfulness
Mindful listening	Mindfulness
Breath counting	Concentration
Mantra meditation e.g. TM	Concentration
Prayer or chanting	Concentration
Tai chi and yoga	Mindfulness

In reality, most people move between each type of meditation while practising mindfulness. At times there may be a wide awareness, especially when practising mindful listening. At others there may be highly focused attention and even absorption, especially when focusing on the breath. A mindful student sitting in class will at times have an open awareness of what is happening around them and what is being taught, and at others will focus intensely on a single problem or task, and then open their attention once more.

It is important not to get uptight about whether we are practising mindfulness or concentration in any given moment, but it can be useful to be aware of what we are practising so that we don't fall into extremes. To help with this, we sometimes ask the participants in our mindfulness courses to do a meditation session with their eyes half open rather than closed, resting their gaze on the ground in front of them without looking at anything in particular. Many people close their eyes anyway, probably partly out of habit but also perhaps showing that they are using mindfulness to block out the present moment and get a nice, relaxed sleepiness going. It is important to realise that this is not mindfulness. It is actually a form of unmindfulness — we call it 'sleepfulness'. And remember that in our neuroplastic use-it-or-lose-it brains, whatever we practise becomes stronger. This includes having a dull attention that is half asleep even while we are nominally awake!

Practising both concentration and mindfulness meditation is like 'sharpening the tool' of attention, which then makes it easier to perform well throughout the day. Like an axe that is sharp, we become much more efficient. This is, in fact, one of the best justifications for taking the time to meditate each day — while there may be some initial resistance to just 'sitting around' rather than being 'productive', knowing that it is making your attention more efficient, and growing your cortex, can be quite motivating. Mindfulness practice becomes an investment in productivity and wellbeing rather than time spent 'doing nothing'.

Attention and memory

For obvious reasons, as we learn to pay attention to what we are doing in each moment, our memory improves. If we don't pay attention to where we put our keys, we are less likely to remember where they are when we next need them. In the same way, any teacher knows that students who pay attention in class tend to perform better. In fact, one of the key things that separates good students from average ones is the ability to remember what is learnt.

In an evolutionary sense, remembering that a sabre-toothed tiger is a threat, or that a certain berry made you sick last time you ate it, was a very useful skill for survival. Indeed, your ancestors are by definition people who learnt this lesson well and learnt it early, because those who didn't remember didn't live long enough to pass on their genes. Fast forward 40,000 years or so, and those students who can remember better than others get selected in a different way — that is, academically. While there are, of course, many other factors that contribute to academic success, people with better memories simply tend to get better grades. They then get into better university courses, tend to get better jobs, and thrive in ways that people with less good memories tend not to.

At its extremes, we see people with photographic and *savant* memory, who can recall vast amounts of detail, and people with amnesia, who cannot recall or encode anything. Most of us are somewhere in the middle of both these extremes. You probably find that you remember some things really well and then at other times forget someone's name or some other thing you need to remember. There are many reasons why this happens. In the rest of this chapter, we examine a couple of them in detail.

Working memory and long-term memory

In order to learn something, students first have to notice and then pay attention to it. This is true whether what they are paying attention to is something happening in the senses (for instance, what you are teaching or what they are reading) or something happening in the mind itself— what we commonly call 'thoughts'. When students pay attention to something they are reading, for instance, parts of the brain associated with vision and language are activated. The prefrontal cortex gets involved, helping them keep their attention on what they are focusing on, and receiving information from the visual and language areas of the brain. This process works optimally when we really focus our full attention on something. Actually, the prefrontal cortex is centrally involved in working or short-term memory, allowing us to hold information in our mind and mentally manipulate it — that is, 'think' about it.

Mind you, there is a trick to memory and paying attention. Trying to force ourselves to pay attention takes a lot of effort and tends to make us tired. This is because we get caught up *thinking about* being mindful rather than actually paying attention. Thinking about paying attention means we get caught up in mental chatter like 'I've got to focus, I've got to be mindful, I've got to remember this'. That's a distraction from really paying attention. When we are just interested and curious, attention and memory work naturally and effortlessly. Think, for example, of times we are doing something we love or looking at something we find fascinating. We don't have to work at remembering the experience — it just seems to happen by itself. They're our mindful moments.

The trap of dividing attention

Short-term, or working, memory is a limited capacity system. A famous experiment done by George Miller at Princeton University in 1956 found that working memory is able to hold only between five and nine things in it at one time. The average is seven, and everyone seems to fall into the five-to-nine range, leading Miller to call the journal article he published his findings in 'The magical number seven, plus or minus two'.[4] He found that information in working memory can be 'chunked' or combined into groups, such as when you remember the entire two- or three-digit area code of a friend's phone number, rather than having to remember the individual digits. The ability to chunk directly relies on being able to hold information — in this case, two or three separate numbers — in working memory for long enough to do the chunking.

And as you would expect, and no doubt know from experience, when we are distracted or dividing our attention between two or more things we do not hold things in mind with enough clarity or for long enough to be able to do this properly. In fact, sometimes we struggle even to remember a single piece of information. No doubt you have been at a party before and have been introduced to someone only to forget their name almost right away. What is happening in moments like this is that our ears hear the sounds that make up the person's name, and the brain areas associated with language decipher the sounds and understand the name, which is then held in working memory (which involves mostly the regions of the prefrontal cortex). But our attention doesn't remain on the name for long enough to encode it in long-term memory (which requires activation of a part of the brain called the hippocampus), maybe because we are focusing on something else such as the next thing the person says or trying to make a good impression and worrying how we are coming across. And then our limited-capacity working memory system gets caught up processing new information (such as what they say next), which literally writes over the top of the old information, and we forget. We won't go into detail about how this process takes place, but what should be obvious is that long-term memory doesn't happen without working memory, and working memory doesn't happen without attention. This is where mindfulness comes in.

Mindfulness and memory

We hope by now you can see how training the mind to pay attention to one thing at a time helps improve memory. On a brain level, research shows that mindfulness practice activates the regions in the brain involved in working memory.[5] And as we know, when we activate or exercise brain regions by using them, they get stronger. So practising mindfulness helps strengthen working memory. This is even true in people under extreme levels of stress, such as military personnel.[6] Interestingly, mindfulness practice also stimulates new nerve cell (neuronal) growth in the hippocampus, improving long-term memory, while worry and default mental activity is associated with a memory centre that operates less effectively and deteriorates faster.[7] Improved working memory capacity means students can encode information better into long-term memory, and can then recall it when they need it. Add to this the fact that mindfulness also reduces stress, which means that our working memory system itself can function better because it is less cluttered with anxious preoccupation, and we start to develop a compelling case for teaching students to pay attention better so they can remember more effectively.

And then we also need to discuss the illusion of multitasking. We already saw in Chapter 2 how attempting to focus on more than one complex task at any one time results in attention switching. And we also saw how there is a brief moment after the neurons in the working memory system have fired where they need to rest and recuperate before they can fire again — the attentional blink. The result is a pause of between a fifth and half a second where no new information can be registered. Anything that happens in this time is simply not noticed. This attentional blink increases when we are stressed. If you think about it, an average 'multitasker' doing their homework with the TV on and chatting on the phone while updating their Facebook profile might switch their attention a few hundred times in an hour. And if they lose half a second each time, this can seriously add up! On the other hand, mindfulness practice has been shown to reduce the duration of the attentional blink and improve the ability to select goal-relevant information from other sensory inputs that are irrelevant or distracting.[8] That is, our ability to filter out what is irrelevant and focus on what is important, improves. This is obviously a very useful skill for students to develop.

In our mindfulness courses we teach people about this illusion of multitasking and the way it reduces efficiency and increases stress. We encourage them to instead practise 'presence of mind' — paying attention to one thing at a time — for a whole week, and observe the difference. They are encouraged to treat it as an experiment. We outline two ways to do this. One is to prioritise, make a list, and do things one at a time, ticking them off as they go. We also encourage them to take a few moments to enjoy the feeling of completing each task before moving on to the next one. So when they are responding to emails they are just responding to emails, and when the phone rings they let it go to voicemail and call the person back when the emails are done. Alternatively, for some people it is better to seamlessly move between tasks — for instance, stop and answer the phone when it rings because the call is important — but to then give their *full* attention to the phone call. This means letting go completely of the email and placing 100 per cent of their focus on the call. Then, once the call has ended, letting go of *it* completely and bringing their full attention back to the email. It can look a little like multitasking but it's not. Instead, it is actually conscious and efficient attention switching.

While at first people seem very worried about trying this out (they're usually concerned that they won't get through the things they need to do) they invariably find that they are actually *more* productive and get much more done than they normally would, and make fewer mistakes and waste less time in the process. They more easily remember to do things, and often realise that some of the things on the list are not actually that important anyway, reducing the sense of pressure. Plus, they tend to finish each day with a sense of completion and mastery that they rarely experienced when trying to juggle twenty things at the same time.

We hope by now you can see that paying attention to what you are doing can help you to remember better. It is by far a more efficient way of learning than dividing your attention between different things and tricking yourself into believing that you are multitasking. Focusing your attention on one thing over a sustained period of time means that you can hold it in working memory long enough to encode it into long-term memory. And when you do this you are also less stressed and miss less information due to attentional blinking. Give it a go and see for yourself.

CHAPTER 7

Learning, mental flexibility and problem solving

Two types of learning

Learning can be looked at in different ways. Memorising things is useful; we can't function well without it. We can memorise the periodic table of physical elements, French grammar, or the times tables, but learning by rote — remembering information, events, facts, figures or screeds of text — is only a superficial expression of what it means to learn. This is learning from the outside-in, in that we are fed information and we just digest it.

There is another form of learning which does not relate so much to information or details as it does to concepts, principles or laws. This kind of learning has to do with understanding, meaning and, potentially, wisdom. It's the kind of learning that makes sense of details and draws meaning out of disparate bits of information.

Let's illustrate this with a simple example. A teacher asks the children to memorise their times tables. Day after day the children have their tables drilled into them and pretty soon they can reel them off with ease. That doesn't mean they know anything about mathematics or how to work out the answers to mathematical problems themselves, but just that they could regurgitate the answer if asked a specific and limited number of multiplication questions. A parrot could probably do the same thing — hence we say that we are merely 'parroting' the answers. A far more useful thing, however, is to learn the laws underpinning how numbers work so that if we were presented with any mathematical problem we could work out the answer. In fact, this is how children in Japan learn multiplication — not by rote learning but through understanding and manipulating a unique mathematical system that then lets them multiply *any* number by any other number, no matter how large. Understanding the laws underpinning mathematics is knowledge we can then adapt to any situation. This involves insight and understanding, not just memory. Such learning is from the inside-out and it's entirely different to rote learning.

What is the experience when we learn by rote? Generally little more than relief at having completed the task. Yes, on a neurological level there are changes taking place in the brain and if we repeat the learning activity then the memory will be stored mostly in the hippocampus. When, on the other hand, we have a moment of real insight — when 'the penny drops' or we have a 'light-bulb moment' as we say — there are a number of other things that take place as well. We experience a moment of clarity and enjoyment. There is an experience of peace and stillness when the mind stops from searching about and comes to rest, having found what it was looking for. It's like finding something that we'd lost — one moment we're restless, the next moment we're at ease.

This learning of concepts, principles or laws from the inside-out is not a new idea. It's an idea as old as philosophy itself. Socrates, for example, was noted for saying that 'all learning is merely recollection' — recalling something that deep down we knew, but didn't know that we knew. If you want to get a sense of how this works, Plato gives a classic example of this in his dialogue, *Meno*, where he teaches an unschooled young man something about geometry and mathematics. What he means by this is that if we look closely and ask the right questions we can come to our own insights and conclusions. If we're attentive, we can recognise the right answer because it will fit, then we can test those conclusions to confirm if they are correct. Our rationality does the working out but the intuition does the knowing. One is busy and the other is quiet. One puts forward all sorts of ideas and propositions and the other sifts and discerns which are relevant and which are not. It's not too different to the approach a scientist takes to making a discovery. As Einstein said, 'The intuitive mind is a sacred gift and the rational mind is a faithful servant. We have created a society that honors the servant and has forgotten the gift.' The specific changes in the brain associated with successful problem solving include heightened activity in the left middle frontal gyrus (associated with executive functioning, attention and motivation) and the left middle temporal gyrus (associated with insight, sound and language).[1] It is also associated with a relaxation response not dissimilar to when we understand a joke.

The effect of bias

When not paying attention we are far more subject to bias in the sense of stepping into situations with a set of unconscious assumptions and pre-conceived ideas. This doesn't allow us to see a situation on its merits. For doctors this is the cause of diagnostic errors.[2] For the student or teacher it is also the source of error and is a major roadblock to our learning. There are two main forms of bias:

Confirmation bias. We interpret things to confirm the assumption we already have about it.

Anchoring bias. We neglect or resist adapting appropriately to subsequent information that suggests alternative possibilities.

It's as if we see some details but get them totally out of perspective and we don't see other details, as if they weren't there. It's not unrelated to 'selective attention'. What would be some examples of this? Racism could be one, in believing that all people of a certain race are stupid or evil. Science is full of bias too, for example, 'The world is flat' or 'After childhood, the brain doesn't change itself' or 'There are tiny little balls of solid matter in the nucleus of atoms'. These beliefs can rule our lives and we might never stop to question them or look again because when young we unconsciously took them on board as facts.

Bias could also be thinking that we are hopeless at something, so that every time we make a mistake we think this just confirms it. In his excellent book, *Blink*, Malcolm Gladwell discusses fascinating research that shows that when African-American students are required to state their ethnicity on an examination paper, their performance drops by 10 per cent simply by stating their race! Furthermore, we don't give any weight to alternate evidence such as positive feedback we may receive or giving ourselves credit for the times when we get it right. This links with 'mindsets' (see Chapter 8).

Biases are not easy to see, especially if we are totally identified with our own thoughts and opinions. The first step to being less affected by bias is to be aware and then to stand back from the thinking mind itself in order to look at it impartially. If we are mindful enough at least we can recognise when we are making an assumption, rather than taking it as a fact — that is, as some objective truth — when it might not be. At least we can then keep the mind open, which allows us to question and discover new things.

Mental flexibility

Unconscious bias is an example of mental or cognitive rigidity. We are often mentally rigid in the food we eat, the clothes we wear, the places we go, the people we meet and the things we are interested in. Just think of your routine this morning as you got up, showered and groomed, dressed yourself and had breakfast. Was how you did it today similar to yesterday (or, indeed, every other day of your life)? We are also generally fairly rigid in the way we work, the way we learn, and the way we teach. This rigidity makes itself obvious when a situation challenges us to do something differently.

When we come to solving a problem we often approach it with a rigid method. A study illustrated this by looking at how people go about solving problems.[3] If you give people a simple problem to solve they will find a way of doing it. If you give them a harder problem they will tend to use the method that worked on the easier one although it might not work so well this time. If you give them increasingly difficult problems, most people will continue to use the method they used initially even though it no longer solves the problem. The end result is generally a fair bit of frustration, wasted time and giving up. In the study, however, participants were then given mindfulness training in a group setting. Although the training didn't explicitly teach problem-solving, mindfulness training led to reduced cognitive or mental rigidity due the tendency to be 'blinded' by experience, meaning that people didn't get blinded by their initial successful experience and subsequently thinking that there was no other or better way to solve the problem. When the initial method they were using no longer worked, or at least didn't work very well, they looked for new and innovative ways of solving it. They were more mentally flexible, looked afresh and thought outside the very small square they had put themselves in.

As young children it is natural to play, explore and be curious about everything that is experienced. You see this in small children when they play outside and touch everything and look at it in wonder, and often — much to the horror of their parents — put it in their mouths. This is sometimes referred to as 'beginner's mind', meaning that each moment is greeted as unique and fresh, with open eyes and an open mind. A famous mindfulness teacher named Suzuki Roshi once said, 'In the beginner's mind there are many possibilities, but in the expert's there are few'. Somewhere along the way most of us learn to learn differently — that is, we make the transition from beginner's to expert's mind — and lose this natural capacity for exploration, curiosity and adaptability which is exactly the kind of capacity that great thinkers have. In the words of Albert Szent-Györgyi, the Hungarian biochemist and 1937 Nobel Prize winner for Medicine: 'Discovery consists of looking at the same thing as everyone else and thinking something different ... A discovery is said to be an accident meeting a prepared mind.' Open-mindedness and mental flexibility are prerequisites for learning, growing, discovering and innovating.

Rewarding process or outcome

A good experiment to do with a class is to present them with the following answer to a mathematics exam question:

$$269 \text{ x}$$
$$23$$
$$\overline{787}$$
$$5380$$
$$\overline{6167}$$

Ask them to work through the problem individually, without talking to each other and without the aid of a calculator. After a minute or two ask them to give the (imaginary) student whose work this is a mark out of 10. If you work through the problem you will note that the student got the question wrong because they didn't carry a 2 on the first line of the multiplication — meaning that the answer should have been 6187. If you do this experiment with a large group you will tend to find a reasonably even spread of marks given from 0 to 9 out of 10. Why? Well, the mark awarded is largely dependent on whether the marker rewarded outcome or process. If it's all about the outcome then you might give 0/10 because the student got the final answer wrong. It's all or nothing. If it's all about the process then the marker might take into account that nearly all of the steps were well performed and the student clearly knew the method for how to do the problem but made a careless mistake. Therefore it's 9/10. If you reward both process and outcome then the mark will be somewhere in between, depending on the weight you give to each. Mind you, if you bought a new car but it didn't start because of some glitch with the ignition, you might feel disposed to give the car manufacturer a 0 rather than 9 out of 10!

What are the implications for the way we teach or learn? Does rewarding the process or outcome have any effect on where our attention goes, our capacity to persevere when challenged or to learn more quickly? Well, it seems that it does, judging by the studies on the learning of children who were either praised for outcome versus effort and process. Dr Tal Ben-Shahar, the noted Harvard author and teacher of Positive Psychology, speaks a lot about this.[4]

If you take a class and give them a relatively easy task you can observe the effect of the teacher's response to the students' work. If the teacher praises the class for the correct outcome then the students will be happy when they get it right. If you then give the same class harder tasks and they don't succeed quickly, nor get the praise they want from the teacher, then most students will get frustrated, won't persevere, and will want to go back to the easier tasks for which they got praise. Thus, making the outcome the only or even main focus of attention isn't necessarily helpful for optimal learning; it can make a challenge appear as a threat and it can lead to an avoidant coping style.

If, on the other hand, you take another class and give them the same relatively easy task, but praise the effort the students make and their learning from mistakes, then the students will tend to enjoy the learning process more. If you then give them a harder task they will be far more likely to enjoy confronting the challenge, want to learn through experience and to persevere because, to them, that is getting it right. As a result, they are likely to learn more quickly and want to extend themselves. Challenge, in this case, is seen more as opportunity and experiment, and mistakes are seen more as learning opportunities rather than assaults on their self-worth or self-esteem. Making mistakes is not a particularly comfortable thing, but when they happen — as they inevitably will — the mindful learner acknowledges and engages with them and therefore learns from them. It may not have been initially pleasant or desirable, but the mistake nevertheless becomes useful.

Performance anxiety

Performance anxiety is not unfamiliar to most of us. Whether we're a student, sportsperson, doctor, leader or teacher, anxiety about the future outcome distracts us from focusing on the present moment process and therefore impedes our performance. A student who becomes anxious about their potential exam results may find themselves almost totally unable to focus on the study they need to do to prepare for those exams. It just doesn't make sense. Being less preoccupied about the potential result helps us to focus on what needs to be done here and now. If we focus on the process, step by step the anxiety reduces but the outcome will look after itself.

Learning and solving problems mindfully

It is becoming increasingly apparent that the improvements in wellbeing associated with mindfulness are also associated with improvements in our level of cognitive functioning.[5] Mindfulness can help both students and teachers in a number of ways.

Before undertaking a task, such as studying a topic at school or home, take a few moments at the outset to practise some mindfulness meditation. This will help to ensure the mind is in the room along with the body.

Remember to start with an open and interested mind and drop the attachment to any particular thoughts you might have about the task or your capacity to do it.

As often as the attention is drawn to thoughts such as, 'I'm hopeless at this' or 'this is too hard' learn not to fight with the thoughts. Just gently notice them and return the attention to the task in front of you. Such ideas are like objects that eclipse or block attention, preventing it from engaging with or illuminating the task. We have more potential than we know, but we will never be able to make use of it unless we learn to free our minds.

Mindfulness will help you recognise your own biases and assumptions when they arise. Note them, consider them, but don't take them for something that they might not be — facts or an accurate reflection of reality.

Being mindful will foster greater comfort with ambiguity. When understanding comes, ambiguity generally dissolves all by itself, but when we're uncomfortable with ambiguity we generally clutch at the first 'answer' to the problem, whether it fits or not. We may feel temporarily more comfortable but such a false sense of security will not solve our problems — quite the opposite.

Mindfulness will help you be open to the connections between what you're learning now and things you've learnt elsewhere. Everything is connected to everything else and life is a lot more interesting when we realise this.

A mindful approach will help you avoid getting stuck. Try things. Have a go. Be prepared to make a mistake and learn from it. Put the results to one side for a moment and enjoy the process. You'll be learning without even realising it.

If something doesn't seem to work or isn't understood then be prepared to let the mind rest on it. Give it a little space. Practise another short meditation or go for a mindful walk and come back to it.

When finished or it's time to move onto another task then do another short meditation to put a little space between activities. It's like mentally cleaning the whiteboard.

CHAPTER 8
Mindsets and learning

If you've been practising mindfulness for a week or two, the chances are that you have already noticed a mental commentary on just about everything that happens, has happened or might happen. Noticing this chatterbox can be frustrating but it is also a sign of increasing mindfulness, because most of the time it was previously hammering away we were oblivious to it. A good metaphor is that most of us have been unmindfully walking around in the dark. For the most part this has been comfortable, but every now and then we bump into something hard with sharp edges or trip over something. Now, after doing even just a little bit of mindfulness practice, it is like a small candle has been lit and all of a sudden we look around and see that there are piles of rubbish, live electrical wires hanging from the ceiling and all manner of obstacles and hazards. Often people report that mindfulness is making their thoughts and neuroses even worse, but actually they are just starting to see — often for the first time — what has been going on in the dark. Now, with some light, we can start to do something about it, or at the very least avoid the most obvious or treacherous obstacles.

Mindsets, mentioned in the last chapter, are a topic of significant importance because they are so subtle we are generally not aware of their presence or the effect they have on how we learn. Carol Dweck is a psychologist who made 'mindset' a common part of educational language.[1,2] According to her there are two main mindsets that we bring to learning (and life in general for that matter): a fixed mindset or a growth mindset.

Fixed mindset

A fixed mindset is both limited and limiting. It is a kind of mental rigidity reflected in how we talk to ourselves and others, including our children and students. When confronted with a challenging task, for a fixed mindset the mental chatter is characterised by thoughts such as 'I can't do that' or 'I don't have enough talent' or 'It's safer not to try' or 'What will people think of me when I fail?'. If we adopt a fixed mindset, we tend to believe that talent and ability cannot be improved, 'at least not by me', even with effort. It's consistent with a notion that we are born with a fixed amount of talent and so there are things we are good at and things we are no good at, end of story. The offshoot is that we tend to avoid challenges in order to avoid the possibility of failure. Failing is not seen as a learning opportunity or as an opportunity for personal growth; it is seen as confirmation of what we already believed about ourselves.

If we become identified with such thoughts about ourselves, challenges will provoke fear and therefore avoidance for the person with a fixed mindset because it's a potential threat to self-worth and self-esteem. We are afraid of being 'discovered' as a fraud. Anything that threatens a closely held thought appears to threaten us if we think we *are* that thought. Fight or flight response, here we come. Mindfulness makes us aware of how identified with, or attached to, our thoughts we are. If we stand back from a thought, even one about ourselves, we may notice that thoughts just come and go by themselves. If a thought comes and goes and we, as the observer of the thought, *don't come and go*, then we cannot be our thoughts. Being able to stand back from thoughts with non-attachment in this way loosens their grip and dissipates a lot of potential fear and anxiety.

Fixed mindsets are not innate. We were not born with them. They are acquired. Imagine being born with a bunch of fixed mindsets. There we are, a baby learning to walk. We fall on our backsides and then say to Mum, 'See, how many times have I told you — I can't walk! Stop asking me to try. I think I'll just sit here for the rest of my life.' There we are at preschool with a set of paints in front of us. We scrawl something on the page, look at it and then say to the teacher, 'Look at what I've produced, it's hopeless. Take those paints away. I'm no Michelangelo. All that paint and paper is just causing me stress!' No, children walk after they have learnt from all the times they tried to balance but failed. They paint, sing, dance and learn as they play.

Children, the younger they are, learn naturally and quickly while the mind is still open and in the present moment. But as time goes on we pick up fixed mindsets from all over the place. They take the fun and the fluency out of learning, make obstacles appear bigger than they really are, and lead us to give up too easily. It's therefore really important that as parents, teachers and friends we are careful with the language we use with others because, consciously or unconsciously, for most of the time we are reinforcing fixed mindsets in others if we hold them ourselves.

From a mindfulness perspective, the fixed mindset monopolises the attention so that it strengthens that mindset such that attention is not allowed to go to the task. If we don't look then we don't learn. Using mindfulness to help us develop a more accepting and less judgmental attitude to the presence of fixed mindsets will help us to gently unhook attention from them when they arise and to engage the attention with what we are trying to master.

Growth mindsets

A growth mindset, on the other hand, believes that intelligence, talent and ability can be developed over time if we are prepared to put in the effort and perseverance required to develop them. A growth mindset can be applied to sport, academic ability, relationships, careers or any other facet of our lives.

A growth mindset sees obstacles as giving rise to a challenge and an opportunity to learn about the task before us but also to grow as a person. Hence a growth mindset does not fear failure but rather sees it as a learning opportunity, or as a chance to improve oneself. High achievers do well not necessarily because they have more talent, resources or opportunity than another person but because they make more focused use of the talent, resources and opportunity they have.

This is not to say that there are not natural differences between individuals in terms of talent and opportunity, but just that we use what we do have either well or badly in large part because of ingrained attitudes and the resulting behaviours. Clearly, a helpful or unhelpful environment will make the learning process easier or harder whether we have a fixed or growth mindset; but with a growth mindset we feel far more empowered to respond to that environment rather than just blame it for our lack of effort or understanding.

Having a growth mindset does not generally mean that achieving is effortless, even for high achievers. On the contrary, achievement is generally on the back of significant effort and perseverance, the kind of effort that the fixed-mindset individual was generally not ready to commit to.

The problem of praise

Praising children or students is fine, but what they are praised for matters a lot. As previously mentioned, research on how we learn shows that being praised for being intelligent or good at something gives a short-term burst of self-esteem but has an unseen number of unwanted and unintended consequences.[3,4] In order to continue to gain praise the child needs to continue to do things at which they are successful, which means doing the easy stuff and avoiding the hard stuff where they might fail or look unintelligent. When challenged and unsuccessful, such children lose motivation and enjoyment quickly, and get distracted. Such children soon adopt a fixed mindset. From a mindfulness perspective, the 'eye is not on the ball' but is instead on the anticipated result.

Children who are praised for making an effort, even when they are unsuccessful, have a different attitude to learning. They are far more likely to welcome challenge, enjoy it and to learn from it as well as to develop resilience in the face of challenge. Such children learn to adopt a growth mindset. These children are not attending to an anticipated result in the future but they are engaged and learning to understand the process in the present moment. The result will look after itself.

Interestingly, the same experiments also show that students who have been praised for intelligence are four times more likely to lie than were students praised for effort when self-reporting their scores on tests. This was largely done to make themselves appear better than they were and therefore be worthy of praise.

In short, being praised for being intelligent tended to foster a fixed mindset and a loss of focus whereas being praised for effort tended to foster a growth mindset and a capacity to focus on tasks.

Mindfulness and mindsets

Mindsets tend to get taken on board early in life. We soak them up without even knowing largely by modelling the adults and teachers around us. However, we can change our mindset at any age if we have the awareness to see it and are prepared to make the effort to foster a different attitude.

Working against ingrained habit is not easy or comfortable. To illustrate this, cross your arms the different way (i.e. the opposite) to how you normally do it. It takes more attention, feels uncomfortable and we want to go back to the way we usually do it. In the same way, changing our patterns of thought will initially feel uncomfortable and unnatural, but with sustained practice it gets easier and easier. To illustrate *this*, cross your arms in the same way you usually do, then the opposite way, then the same again, repeating this a number of times and observing what happens. Soon the new, opposite way of doing it becomes less foreign. If you did this often enough, the new way of crossing your arms would actually come to feel comfortable.

The first step in changing a habit is awareness. If we can't see it then we can't change it. Mindfulness helps us to develop a growth mindset by:

- recognising the telltale signs of a fixed mindset when it arises, such as fear, avoidance, mental agitation, inattention or the desire to lie about test results
- noticing the chatterbox — not just the fact that there *is* a commentary in our minds but also the *nature* of that commentary
- standing back from our thoughts to see them not as facts but just as thoughts
- helping us exercise more choice about whether or not to act on and reinforce certain thoughts
- keeping our attention on the activity we're trying to learn about or master by engaging with it more fully and unhooking the attention from self-consciousness about outcome, performance and failure
- reducing stress in order to liberate the areas of the brain required for learning
- choosing language and responses that encourage a growth mindset.

Changing from a fixed to a growth mindset

One of the classic traps in changing mindsets is that the fixed mindset is likely to start sabotaging things right at the outset. You may have even had the following thought: 'Oh no, I'm a fixed mindset kind of person and that's that. If only I had a growth mindset I could change.' Making the transition takes a little bit of faith that change is possible, but that faith won't change anything unless it is backed up by effort and patient practice. That's where mindfulness comes in. Then we can take a few steps towards changing mindsets a whole lot more easily and successfully.

Carol Dweck breaks down her approach to changing mindsets into four steps which are summarised below.[5]

Step 1: Learn to hear your fixed mindset 'voice'

Notice the nature of the chatterbox, especially as you approach a challenge or learning opportunity. Does it self-sabotage, deride, deflect and avoid? Does it get defensive and justify potential failure? Does it distort what others say?

Step 2: Recognise that you have a choice

We have a choice as to whether or not we acknowledge the chatterbox. Will our attention and energy be given to avoidance, criticism and justification — again — or will our attention and energy be directed to the challenge? Notice if the chatterbox tries to deflect the attention and undermine the effort. Reaffirm your growth mindset choice.

Step 3: Talk back to it with a growth mindset voice

Although talking to ourselves is not generally part of a mindfulness approach, once we create some space in our minds and begin experiencing thoughts as thoughts (rather than facts) we can decide to give attention to the kinds of thoughts and behaviours we want to affirm. That is, we can simply stop following or resisting unhelpful thoughts and urges, and begin identifying with more useful ones. If we do this often enough, the new thought will start to hardwire itself into the brain through neuroplasticity. For example, as you approach a challenge, affirm growth mindset thoughts such as:

'I'm not sure I can do it now, but I think I can learn to with time and effort.'

'Most successful people had failures along the way.'

'If I don't try, I automatically fail. Where's the dignity in that?'

If you hit a setback:

'Basketball wasn't easy for Michael Jordan, and Albert Einstein actually failed maths at school. They had a passion, put in tons of effort and learnt how to focus their attention.'

If you face criticism:

'If I don't take responsibility, I can't fix it. Let me listen — however painful it is — and learn whatever I can.'

Step 4: Take the growth mindset action

A thought that is not reinforced by our behaviour will not change anything. Follow through and learn from the experiment of acting in a way that is consistent with a growth mindset. Then reflect on which kind of mindset will serve you best in life — fixed or growth?

CHAPTER 9

Resilience and managing stress

It's one thing to notice how stress affects us mentally, emotionally, functionally and socially; it's another to manage it well. In this chapter we look at stress in more detail, including how it impacts us in various educational situations, and what mindfulness can offer us in terms of managing stress better and developing resilience.

The what and why of stress

'Stress' is a commonly used word to cover a multitude of sins. So what is 'stress'? In its natural sense, it's an adaptive response aimed at saving our life in a present-moment, threatening situation. In modern life it has also come to mean much else besides, such as the wide variety of unpleasant emotional states we experience when anxious, a state of mind such as agitation or confusion, or an inability to focus. Sometimes it is used to describe burnout, irritability or being preoccupied in the middle of the night.

Stress is defined by some experts as a perceived inability to cope. If the perceived demands are high, and our perceived resources are low, we will experience a mismatch between the two such that we expect to be overcome by the situation (threat) in front of us. The important word here is *perceived*. Perception is everything. As the ancient Greek philosopher Epictetus said, 'Men [or women] are disturbed not by things, but by the view which they take of them.' How we see an event determines if it is a good thing, a bad thing or a complete non-event. Shakespeare was onto it too when he wrote, 'There is nothing either good or bad, but thinking makes it so.' It is not the event that determines the response but our perception or evaluation of it. For example, let's say a mouse runs under the table at a family dinner; one person sees a monster, one sees a source of annoyance and one, probably the five-year-old, sees a potential pet. Likewise, a teacher gives a poor mark on an assignment with a whole lot of comments attached — one student sees evidence that they are a complete and utter failure, one sees an outrageous injustice, one sees a reality check, and one sees an opportunity to learn something.

If we are not really paying attention we will miss the fact that the mind quickly and automatically projects attitude, anticipation, assumption and expectation onto events, many of which may have nothing to do with the actual merits of the situation. If we reflect on the above example of the poor grade, having the mental space to perceive the event in a way that we can learn from it is far more conducive to future success than reacting negatively.

As far as the body's role in the stress response is concerned, the body will just do whatever the mind tells it to do — similar to the relationship between a car and the driver. Switched on when it needs to be, stress has an important and natural role to play. The physical fight or flight response can be likened to a turbo-charge of energy. It's pretty good for getting us out of a life-threatening situation as well as lifting us out of apathy and inertia. A tiger walks into a room, the heart races to get extra blood to the heart and muscles as they ready for action. Blood is diverted from low priority areas like the gut and skin to the muscles. This is why digestion shuts down, the mouth goes dry and we go pale. Fuel rapidly pumps into the bloodstream, ready for the muscles to burn. We breathe fast to get oxygen on board to help us to burn the fuel. Our blood gets thicker to help stop bleeding should we be injured in the fight ahead of us. Immune cells activate for the same reason. We sweat to keep ourselves cool while we exert ourselves getting away from the tiger, and so on.

This can sound like anxiety but in a situation like this it's not — it's an activation response to help us do things we can't ordinarily do. It's when we activate this response when we don't actually need it — such as worrying a day, a week or a month before an exam — that it's experienced as anxiety (stress). In this situation the chemicals driving the response, such as adrenaline and cortisol, are pumping out but they have nowhere to go and nothing useful to do. The heart is racing, we're breathing fast, we are pale, sweaty and shaky, and we feel a little nauseated because the gut has shut down. Unfortunately, when worrying, the tiger is in the imagination, not in reality. Responding with fight (frustration), flight (avoidance) or freezing (procrastination) is not useful in such situations. It makes it difficult for our brains to work well, which affects learning, memory, sleep and health. The irony is that the fight or flight response is not even useful in the exam room. Yes, a bit of stress is better than apathy and laziness, but an exam is not a tiger that's going to eat us. Because of our fears about potential results we perceive that it is. Worrying about the result is a distraction from the exam. Be alert (mindful), not alarmed (stressed)!

Resilience

Resilience refers to a capacity to spring back after being stretched, tested or put under pressure. Sometimes it also refers to being able to be buoyant under trying circumstances. You see it in how people cope well during and after natural disasters. We will all be stretched at various times in our lives as we meet challenges that test our capacities and resources. The further we go in our educational and occupational lives the more we are likely to be stretched.

Resilience is becoming a more commonly used word, especially in the context of personal development. To know what might enhance resilience we first need to look at the things that undermine it. These include:

Rigidity. If we don't learn to bend under pressure we will break. A brittle, dead branch of a tree will break in a high wind whereas a live green one will bend. Flexibility therefore enhances resilience whether that is flexibility in the way we think, or knowing when to give ourselves some time off.

Non-acceptance. Not being able to accept things the way they are increases stress and prevents us from adapting to a situation. Mindful acceptance is about engaging and is not the same as resignation.

Being unhealthy. If we are not physically or emotionally well we have very little left in reserve for when demands increase.

Having no functional reserve. If we stretch time, energy and resources to the limit, and don't leave a bit in reserve for the unexpected, then it takes very little adversity to put the system into crisis.

Flexibility, acceptance, wellbeing, functional reserve — this is where mindfulness comes in. Let's now look at how mindfulness might help us to enhance resilience and manage stress.

Workload and procrastination

Workload varies at school and university but in general terms it increases the further we get into our education careers and the closer we get to exams and assignment deadlines. What are some of the main ways we can increase workload for ourselves?

Procrastination

It is amazing how we spend so much time thinking about a task that we use up all the available time to do it. Procrastination is generally fed by thoughts such as, 'There's so much to do', 'Where do I start?', 'What if I fail?', 'I don't want to study, I wish I was doing something else'. Then we get angry with ourselves for not getting on with it, and then more anxious because we have even less time to do whatever it is we need to do. Then we might start to wish even more passionately that we were somewhere else, or get depressed because we don't seem to have any control over our minds and behaviour, and then the world feels as if it's closing in, and then we fight with ourselves which only makes it worse, and on it goes in a never-ending spiral.

Where's our attention in this process? On a whole lot of internal, circular dialogue. Where does the attention really need to be? On the work we need to get on with. Where is all the energy going? Into a whole lot of inertia, frustration and self-loathing. What can we do? Try a circuit breaker. A walk or a jog or a shower can be good. It can help us to settle and then get our attention engaged again with the senses. Some mindfulness meditation can help us to stand back from the thoughts and emotions for long enough to get a bit of distance and freedom from them. Then we can gently choose one priority and engage the attention with it. We can also try not fighting with ourselves and our state of inertia, but instead change our attitude to it. We can just acknowledge that it's not an uncommon thing to experience, it's understandable, but it's not going to get us very far. It's not so much a matter of trying to control all those negative thoughts and feelings but rather learning not to be so controlled by them.

Avoidance, denial and time wasting

In procrastination there is generally a fair amount of tension as one part of us wants to get on with the work but another part doesn't. With avoidance, denial and time wasting there is often a lack of tension and motivation. We don't acknowledge the work that is there to be done. We ignore it and maybe pretend to ourselves that it's not even there as we find a multitude of other things to do. 'I'll just see what's happening on Facebook first', 'I'll just see what's in the fridge', 'I'll just call so-and-so', 'I'll just lie down on my bed and have a little nap'. Of course the workload doesn't go away but what we have done is eat up the time available to do it until we don't have enough time. What seemed like a good way of avoiding stress in the beginning has amplified it enormously when the truth finally dawns on us. What can we do about it? Recognise when we're fooling ourselves; stop and take some time to practise being mindful; sit down and sort out our priorities and what is going to work well for us in the long run.

Being inefficient and disorganised

When we're stressed we become inefficient. It's not just that we don't focus well, we also jump from one thing to another, losing track and being disorganised. This amplifies the workload because although we are 'getting on with it' we take so much longer to get the same amount of work done than if we were more efficient and organised. Attention equals efficiency. We save a lot of time by stopping before we start, having a work plan, and then following through with it. When the mind distracts you during the work, notice this and re-engage it. When you're anxiously trying to do it all at once then stop, and take one step at a time. Hasten slowly.

Working without perspective

When stressed we often think that some things are more important than they are, such as focusing on the minutiae, to the point that we don't give the important stuff the attention it deserves. It's a case of getting things out of perspective. The 'little picture' looks big and the big picture isn't seen at all. One aspect of this is 'trying to know everything'. This happens a lot in students who are disposed to perfectionism. When we study without a clear perspective of what is most and least important then we get very little return for our time. What can we do about it? Ask for perspective. Stop and, before undertaking a task such as revising for an exam or beginning an assignment, ask ourselves questions like, 'What is most and least important?'. Gaining perspective is one of our important executive functions and it works best when we are mindful.

Multitasking

This has been explored but suffice to say here, multitasking is associated with being more stressed and pressured when we work. It is also associated with inefficiency, remembering less and understanding things in less depth. Part of the allure of multitasking is that it creates an appearance of getting more done in a given amount of time. The solution? When you notice you are multitasking, stop and focus again on priority number one.

Exams

Almost everyone assumes exams have to be stressful, and not just the exams themselves but also the weeks and months leading up to them. Why? If we're extremely anxious about the outcome, if our minds have backed us into a corner by assuming there is only one result conducive to happiness and anything else is disaster, if we're constantly comparing ourselves to others and their marks, if we assume that stress is the best possible and only driver of performance, or if we're measuring our self-worth by the mark received on an exam, then we've created the perfect state of mind to make exams stressful.

Studies show that students who are most anxious during exams perform well below their potential because the area of the brain (the prefrontal cortex) that's meant to be processing information largely through the operation of the short-term memory is instead clogged up with worries about how we are going to go.[1,2] It seems strange that we could worry about the outcome of an event such as an exam to the extent that we can't get on with it. Here are a few tips on what to do about it.

See 'Workload and procrastination' (p. 88). Re-read this section and practise everything outlined.

Practise not getting ahead of yourself. We can worry a lot about the future and may have already decided that our life is washed up even before we have lived it. The exam will come in its own time, not before.

Cultivate an accepting attitude. Unhook attention from the endless stream of thought telling us how terrible it will be if x, y or z happens. Life will have its ups and downs but it will take a lot of pressure off if you can accept that. See the result, whatever it ends up being, as an opportunity to learn not just about the subject matter you are being examined on but, more importantly, about ourselves.

Stress is not the best driver of performance. If you've never questioned whether stress is the best and only driver of performance then stress will be inevitable. Students often blindly take on this assumption and then talk to each other in a way that keeps feeding that belief. The only way that stress improves performance is because it lifts us out of apathy and inertia. After that, it's the attention and focus we bring to the task that drives performance, not the stress.

Practise mindfulness. You can practise mindfulness both informally and formally.

Informal (during study and exam times): This includes all the things that have been said before, particularly when the attention goes off, gently bring it back ...

Formal (meditation): The mind may think, 'I don't have time to practise meditation, I've got too much to do.' That's a bit like a woodcutter saying, 'I don't have time to sharpen my axe, I've got too much wood to cut.' Those few minutes sharpening the axe will save a huge amount of time. It is an investment, not an expenditure. If we're not practising mindfulness we can be pretty confident that we're practising unmindfulness.

Deadlines

Exams are not the only potential source of stress. A deadline for an assignment or thesis can cause considerable anxiety and pressure. Such pressure can be further aggravated by procrastination, perfectionism and overly worrying about the result. Clearly, being organised and focused will help enormously and getting on to the task early rather than leaving it to the last minute will mean there is generally plenty of time to do what we need to.

When deadlines build up we often feel so distracted by our internal dialogue that we find it hard to get on-task. Thoughts such as, 'I'll never get through it all' or 'Why have I left it to the last moment again?' don't tend to help. The big issue is not to waste precious time and energy going over the past or worrying about the future — only *now* matters. In order to successfully manage your time:

- Sit and settle.
- Get what you need in front of you.
- Methodically make a plan for the time you have.
- Unless there is a major reason not to, stick to the plan.
- Focus on priority one.
- When you notice the attention going off, refocus.
- Let waves of worry come and go without reacting to them.
- 'Surf' urges to check Facebook or otherwise procrastinate and avoid the work.
- When it's time to rest and get some sleep, stop, sit, settle and sleep — your work will be waiting for you in the morning.

Managing expectations

The expectations we put on ourselves, or the ones we take on from others, can put an enormous amount of stress on situations and, paradoxically, impair our capacity to meet those expectations. There is nothing wrong with aiming high and using the best of our abilities, but the kind of expectations that create the most stress and the greatest potential for disappointment are those that become rigid and inflexible. For some, such as overseas students or students whose parents have made significant sacrifices to put them through their education, the expectations from parents can be the greatest. They might be well intended but they might not be helping.

What drives the kind of expectations that create the most stress and potentially impair performance? Generally, narrow assumptions about what we think will make us happy. Mindfulness can teach us to work towards the goals we set for ourselves, step by step, but without the rigid ideas that create a prison for ourselves or someone else. Expectations are only thoughts and they have no more and no less power to move us than the attention we give them and the extent to which we become attached to them.

There is also another problem. When expectations don't match reality there will be an inevitable come down; call it a reality check. Such examples could be when expectations don't match ability, motivation, resources or time. Yes, we can make the best of what we have if we work well, efficiently and in a focused manner, but reality will not be denied.

Learning from failure

If we don't learn from failure we can feel confident we will have another opportunity to soon enough because we will be destined to make the same mistake again. The bigger the failure the greater the potential for learning. A mindful response to failure is to:

- be able to sit with, and be open to, the discomfort
- acknowledge the failure, turn the attention to it rather than avoid it, learn from it and then move on
- take a bigger view of life with its ups and downs (this too will pass)
- not measure our self-worth by one apparent success or failure in one particular episode of life.

What makes failure so fear provoking is that it tends to threaten a closely held idea about ourselves such as, 'I'm great' or 'I'm capable', which is generally a cover for the idea sitting just underneath it such as, 'I'm hopeless' or 'I'm incompetent'. Drop the attachment to the idea, whatever it happens to be, and the threat goes away. Being comfortable with being human takes away a lot of fear. What is left in its place is a clearer mind that is more receptive and open to learning from the mistakes that might have led to the failure in the first place.

Rudyard Kipling hit the nail on the head in his poem *If*, which was written to his son when he turned sixteen. Here are a few lines from it, with the third and fourth, interestingly, being inscribed over the doorway leading onto the centre court at Wimbledon.

> *If you can dream — and not make dreams your master;*
> *If you can think — and not make thoughts your aim;*
> *If you can meet with Triumph and Disaster*
> *And treat those two impostors just the same.*

CHAPTER 10

Emotional development

Beginning in late childhood and continuing until early adulthood, the prefrontal cortex becomes more active, allowing us to think more abstractly and to imagine the future and recall the past more easily, as well as regulating our emotions and inhibiting our impulses. This happens earlier for females than males. This is why women commonly seem to 'mature' earlier than men, and why young men often have issues with impulse control and aggression.

During this period, peer and romantic relationships start to replace family relationships in terms of importance for adolescents. Responsibilities and pressures mount, and young people can easily become overwhelmed. They are particularly prone to this early on, before the prefrontal cortex has fully developed.[1] One of the paradoxes of adolescence is that the same brain structure that allows things to become much more complicated for a young person becomes developed enough to open up new worlds, but is not immediately strong enough to deal with the intense new emotions that come with this.[2] It is therefore important that young people learn to use mindfulness to navigate this often bumpy stage of emotional development.

We cannot understand or develop any aspect of ourselves without paying attention, and emotions are no different. Mindfulness can help us to observe our emotional states and to respond appropriately rather than simply reacting to them. In fact, the prefrontal cortex, which we have already discussed in detail in Chapter 2, is also centrally involved in regulating emotions and inhibiting impulses. This chapter is about using mindfulness to more effectively manage and respond to emotional states. Through learning how to do this, we become more effective human beings — by enhancing our 'judgment, character and will', as William James put it. If we don't learn how to work with our emotions, it will impair our lives in many ways and reduce our capacity to learn, remember, be creative, function under pressure and relate to others.

Emotional regulation

Emotion is all about energy. Like fire, if we understand it and work with it wisely it serves us well. If we don't, it can burn down the house. To be alive is to have emotions. All day long, we experience an ever-changing array of different emotional states. Most of the time this variability is not a problem. We simply experience the play of emotions in our minds and bodies and continue to do the things that need to be done. At times, however, we get overwhelmed by emotion and find it hard to focus on anything else. This can make it hard to function. It can also create lots of problems for us if we identify with our emotions and vent them at others, or experience resentment (which is like drinking poison and waiting for the other person to die!). Prolonged anger has even been found to make our DNA age faster so whether or not we harm someone else with it, we are certainly harming ourselves.[3] We therefore need to be able to manage our emotions.

There are different ways to do this. Broadly speaking, when we experience a particular emotion that we don't want, we can do one of two things. Firstly, we can change the way we think about the particular situation so that its significance is altered. For instance, if we really want to win a game but instead get beaten, we can tell ourselves 'it is just a game'. This is called *reappraisal*. Alternatively, we make sure the disappointment does not show on our face or in our voice. This is called *suppression*. Research shows that people who suppress emotions tend to become unable to fully experience *any* emotion, whether pleasant or unpleasant, and are more susceptible to a range of problems such as anxiety, depression and heart disease.[4] This makes a lot of sense given what we have said so far about mindfulness — specifically that trying not to think about or feel something inherently focuses our attention on it, tends to amplify it, and takes a lot of energy to suppress it. As soon as we stop trying to not experience it, it tends to pop right up, bigger and badder than before. As the saying goes, 'What you resist, persists'.

Research shows that reappraisal is much healthier. It avoids the psychological and physical problems associated with suppression, and turns out to be a much better way of regulating emotions. However, the problem with reappraisal is that when we change the way we think about something and the situation changes (since everything is always changing anyway), we have to repeat the process over and over again. We have to keep on changing our thinking to deal with situations that cause us distress.

Working with emotions mindfully

There is another way — a more mindful way — to work with emotion. Mindfulness turns out to be a third, distinct type of emotion regulation that is healthier than either reappraisal or suppression.[5] Mindful emotion regulation, as we have already discussed, simply means allowing the emotion to come and go without reacting to it. Instead of trying to *control* the emotion by fighting with it or suppressing it, we learn not to be *controlled by* the emotion. We practise standing back from it and observing it with acceptance and without criticism. This requires anchoring our attention on the body or something happening in the senses (and therefore in the present moment) so that we don't get swept away by the flood of emotional energy. It also requires accepting the thoughts and feelings that make up the emotional experience, rather than reacting to them or letting them drive our behaviour. In this way, we are able to continue doing whatever we are doing, despite having strong emotions. We start having our emotions rather than them 'having' us.

It can be reassuring to know that in any moment we are experiencing an emotion, it is already leaving us, rather than coming at us. This is generally not well understood and leads us to thinking we need to change or fix certain emotions in order to function, rather than just letting them be there and getting on with things. The paradox is that they will settle by themselves if we allow them to, but we don't allow them to settle if we keep stirring up the muddy water by trying to do something about them.

Obviously, there are certain people or situations that make particular emotions likely. But what often gets overlooked is the fact that it is the way we *perceive* situations that dictates whether we will react negatively or positively. If a student sits at their desk and resents a piece of work they are doing — telling themselves that it is irrelevant, getting frustrated that they have to do it and thinking about how much nicer it would be to go outside or text a friend — they are likely to experience a great deal of stress. In contrast, if they just accept that it is a necessary part of their studies, and approach the task with an attitude of curiosity about what new things could be learnt, they will be less stressed and will learn much better. Resentment wastes time and energy and impedes learning. Recognising that it is perception that shapes our emotional experience lets us respond more effectively to our emotions.

Mindfulness gives us a way to simply observe what is happening without getting caught up in it or resisting it. The best thing we can do when we experience strong emotions is to notice their presence in our mind and their effect on the body, bringing an attitude of openness and acceptance to them, making room for them to be there as they are, and simply keeping our attention on what we are doing. At times, this can be pretty hard to do. But if we practise, it gets easier.

An important recent study on secondary school students showed that not only were the rates of acceptability of the mindfulness program high for the students, but children who participated in the mindfulness intervention reported fewer depressive symptoms post-treatment compared to students who didn't participate the program. At a three month follow-up, the mindfulness group also showed lower stress and greater wellbeing. Importantly, the degree to which students in the mindfulness group practised their mindfulness skills was associated with better wellbeing and less stress at the follow-up.[6]

In Exercise 9, 'Communicating with awareness' (p. 231) we outline a very effective method of responding mindfully to emotions. Exercise 8, 'Working mindfully with emotions' (p. 225), is also very effective and introduces the vital aspect of curiosity (as discussed below) as a way to stamp out reactivity.

The vital component in working mindfully with emotions is *curiosity*. This is what makes mindfulness really work, especially when responding to strong emotional experiences. The reason for this is that most people tend to think they are relating to their experiences with acceptance and openness, but are actually fostering a subtle resistance to them. It is tempting to 'accept' an emotion in the hope that it will go away. This is a trap that can even snare people who have been practising mindfulness for many years. However, bringing genuine curiosity to our experience circumvents any resistance: we can't be genuinely curious about something and at the same time try to get rid of it or ignore it. This is why curiosity is a central part of mindfulness practice. And, of course, it is quite a useful quality for students to have when they are trying to learn!

Once the peak of the emotion has passed, along with the urge to do something to get rid of it, we can again focus fully on whatever we were doing before the emotion appeared. In fact, we may even find that we have additional energy to put into the activity — especially if the emotion was strong anger. In this way, emotions can become useful allies for us rather than enemies. Changing our attitude toward them in this way further enhances our ability to accept them when they arise, rather than identifying with them or frantically trying to get rid of them.

We can work with thoughts in a similar way. When we need to get some space from them, we can centre ourselves by not being caught up in them and focusing on our breathing for a time. Then, once we have a little distance from the thoughts, we simply let them go past, like products on an assembly line, while we become the quality controller. We must be careful not to become like a harsh critic, judging or reacting to the thoughts. Instead we simply allow thoughts that don't serve us to come and go, and when we see a thought that may actually lead to something useful, we give it energy by paying attention to it. If we can help people learn to do this when they are young, it is a skill that will stand them in good stead for the rest of their lives.

Of course, it is important to acknowledge that we cannot always maintain the mental balance necessary to work with our emotions in this skillful way. In moments where it is not possible to get *mental* distance from our thoughts and emotions, it may be necessary to make *physical* distance. This may entail leaving the situation and taking 'time out' to calm down. However, this is different to avoiding difficulties, because there is an intention to return to face (and work through) the situation once the intensity of the emotional reaction has subsided. Giving ourselves permission to do this — and developing the presence of mind to know when this is necessary — is an important part of mindfulness.

CHAPTER 11

Communication and relationships

You know that awkward moment when someone is speaking to you and you are smiling and nodding and kind of following the thread but really thinking about what you are going to say next — or even something else entirely — and then there's that awkward pause, where you know you're meant to respond but don't really know what the question was? Or maybe you post things online without thinking, often with disastrous consequences? These are examples of unmindful communication, where the body is in one place, doing one thing, while the mind is somewhere else entirely. As we have explored so far in this book, operating in this way tends to reduce performance, increase stress and cause a range of other problems. It can also impair communication, damage relationships and even land us in hot water. What's more, we have to communicate effectively to teach effectively.

You are hopefully also familiar with the experience of talking to someone and having their full, undivided attention. Of having someone *really* get what you are saying, understanding not just the words you say but also your tone and body language, almost as if they are tapping in to some much deeper part of you, and hearing that. And you probably know what it is like when someone clearly expresses exactly what you are thinking or feeling, by finding the right word for the occasion or mood. It is moments such as these that show us what communication *can* be, if we really bring our full selves to the endeavour, that is.

This chapter is about *interpersonal* mindfulness. Mindfulness tends to start off being about us, but if it doesn't ultimately become about our connection with others and the world around us, we are missing the point. Actually, our relationships with others always reflect our relationship with ourselves. And if we can't relate well to ourselves we can't relate well to others.

Communicating mindfully

Mindful communication begins when we start bringing presence to our interactions with each other. It begins with a recognition that the exact same habits we have begun noticing in ourselves when we practise mindfulness also show up in our interactions with others. The default mode of labelling and judgment, reactivity and automatic responding, and liking and disliking that we do with ourselves also colours the way we listen and speak.

If we pay attention, we start noticing how often our attention is elsewhere while we are 'communicating' with others. We notice the layers of judgment and expectations through which we relate to those around us and the tendency to switch off, daydream, judge, criticise or plan what to say next once the other person has finished speaking. This is the automatic pilot of our interactions. To bring this to life, start paying attention to your own interactions and noticing how difficult it is to just be present with people while they talk to us, how uncomfortable it is to be silent and just be with them, and how overwhelming the urge is to fill any silence with talking.

Also notice the effect this has on your ability to really connect with people, to understand them, to truly hear them and allow them to express themselves. Or to really say what is important to you rather than just mindlessly talking. Notice how this affects your teaching, your parenting, your relationships with your partner and friends. Perhaps reflect on the ways this might contribute to some of the misunderstanding and conflict in our schools and universities, families and society at large. Begin to wonder what it might be like if we all started communicating with more mindfulness.

So what can we do about this? To begin with, we can make a commitment to developing mindful communication strategies. We can commit to really listening to others when they speak, noticing what they are really saying, as well as tuning in to how they are saying it. If we need to be somewhere else then by all means we can politely excuse ourselves, but if we are listening to someone then why not just listen? And when we speak, we can make a commitment to speaking our truth as best we can, seeking to express ourselves authentically.

When we do this, people start responding to us differently. Bit by bit, interaction by interaction, our relationships have the chance to improve and our connections deepen. In turn, our relationship with ourselves tends to deepen and become more loving. We can quickly find ourselves in a positive feedback loop: when we really listen to and honour ourselves, we can bring this to others, increasing the likelihood that they will start to interact with us in that way, which helps us in turn do it even more with them. Finally, we can find ourselves in an ongoing practice of interpersonal mindfulness, where each moment of interaction supports our ongoing presence and awakening to what is deepest and most true within us.

While this may sound rather idealistic, it is also extremely practical. We can start experiencing this more right now, in this very moment — which is, of course, the only place where mindfulness ever happens! We can simply extend what we have been exploring already so far in this book.

The rest of this chapter lays out a number of mindful communication practices, with an invitation to have a play with them and notice the effects on our relationships. As a very famous mindfulness teacher (the first, actually) once said, 'Don't take any of this on face value — try it out and see how it works for you.'

Mindful listening

Once we learn to listen mindfully, for instance to the sounds around us, we can begin listening more attentively to others. The exercises mentioned below will help you practise mindful listening and communication. In the rest of this chapter, we will outline some of the basic principles.

Exercise 9, 'Communicating with awareness' (p 231) is a detailed exercise to practise mindful listening, while Exercise 11a, 'Multitasking — communicating' (p. 235) is a mindfulness communication practice that requires two people and helps you develop the ability to really hear what your partner is saying and really speak your truth rather than just talking mindlessly. Exercise 3, 'Tuning in to your surroundings', (p. 208) also works with mindful listening.

When we start mindfully tuning in to environmental sounds we get to see how pervasive the default mode of listening is. We can start observing ourselves going between listening to the actual sounds and 'listening' to our internal monologue. We can notice the tendency of the mind to label and judge what we hear, and to seek out and fixate on certain sounds. And as with any mindfulness practice, this awareness provides us with an opportunity to redirect our attention from our default-mode mental projections and reconnect with what is actually happening in each moment. We can start to learn about the ways our habits of unmindfulness impair our ability to listen and communicate.

Once we have had some practice listening mindfully, we can start bringing this to our communication. We can begin noticing the ways that we get caught up in 'listening' to the thoughts and judgments about what is being said or the person saying it, rather than paying attention to the actual words and non-verbal communication. When we are listening on automatic pilot we have often formulated a response before the person has even finished speaking, or we judge what is being said, or wander off into thoughts only tangentially related (if at all) to the conversation. Just as when we are practising mindfulness alone, the moment these habits are noticed we are no longer caught up *in* them but have woken up to the fact that although we may not have been present we are the *observer* of the mental habit and not the habit itself. This begins, again, with bringing our full attention to what we can hear with our ears rather than our thoughts. We can also tune into the sensations of the body, and come back to these over and over whenever we find ourselves momentarily caught up in reacting or fixating on a particular part of the communication experience. From here, it is about applying effort to refocus our attention on the conversation. This will require us at times to consciously release tension from our body and our mind, to take a moment to just breathe and *be*, without trying to achieve anything in particular. It is this stepping out of autopilot and dropping into awareness that makes real listening possible: it is actually far easier to relax into listening than it is to force our attention to fixate there.

If communicating mindfully, we can seek to hear more than just the words being said. We can tune in to the tone of the other person's voice, their posture and other non-verbal components of the conversation. Remember that 80 per cent of communication is non-verbal and very often we get a far better idea of what a person really means by their emotion and physical gestures rather than what they say. Words convey the content, while emotion is more directly expressed through prosody (rhythm, structure and intonation of speech), pauses, intensity, rate and vocal tone, as well as posture, facial expressions and even intuition. Start with focused listening — to meaning and emotion — and when this becomes comfortable, widen your attention to take in the whole conversation, including the overall direction and flow. Tune in to the overall pattern and as you do so, notice how this allows you to better tune in to whomever you are interacting with. At first it might seem strange because it is not our habitual way but it gets easier and more natural every time we practise it.

Of course, notice any reactions you have to what is being said, but simply note these in the same way that you have been noting reactions to bodily sensations, sounds and thoughts in the meditation practices. It may take some practice to accept or let go of these reactions, but if you have been practising even a little bit, you will know by now that it is possible. Also start listening out for what is *not* being said. Just as we can listen to environmental sounds and the silent space between them, it is possible to start tuning in to what is being communicated both via words and silence. You have no doubt experienced moments with people where both of you sat in silence and yet communicated deeply, perhaps with your gaze or even just with your presence.

When we practise in this way, listening to others fully becomes a meditation practice itself. By bringing this awareness to listening, you can literally 'listen' the other person into awareness, providing a space for them to be truly heard, where they can authentically express themselves. In fact, through doing this, we can make the transition from listening to actually *hearing*. This is a very useful distinction to make. Think about it.

Mindful speech

Just as we can listen more fully by stepping out of the automatic pilot of communication, it is possible to begin speaking more mindfully. This refers to speaking our truth, as best we can in any given moment, and simultaneously being aware of what we are saying and what it is like to say it. In the beginning, as is generally the case with mindfulness, it is useful to slow things down a bit. This allows us to step out of the usual habits of chattering away with semiconscious speech. Take a breath — a deliberate pause — before speaking.

We can check in with ourselves about what we are about to say and why we have chosen to say this, out of all the possible things we could offer with our speech to this moment. What is our motivation? If it doesn't feel right then perhaps it's better not to say it. What is the feeling tone inside us? What thoughts are about to be expressed? Recognise how, when we speak with expectations or attachment to certain outcomes, we are not fully present in that moment to our thoughts or what is happening around us. Often we are speaking out of pre-programmed habits and automatic pilot, rather than responding to the situation in front of us with freshness and creativity. And then, after we have spoken, we can pause again and check in with ourselves. What did it feel like to say that? Did it come out as intended? Was that our truth, in this moment, as best we understand it? And what response did we get from the other person? How did they receive what we said? As we engage in this reflective process, notice how speaking and listening are inseparable, like two sides of the same coin. With time the whole process refines itself and there tends to be less disconnection between what is happening on the inside and what we express on the outside.

Obviously, we can never fully express what we mean. Speech, like discursive thought, is inherently limited and only ever approximates our intentions and experiences. All we can do is endeavour in each moment to express ourselves as clearly and authentically as we can, and then be honest with ourselves about whether we are actually doing this well. We can also seek to become more aware of the effects of what we say on others. This is one of the hallmarks of emotional intelligence.

Communicating with intention

When we practise in this way, both listening and speaking — indeed communicating generally — become mindfulness practices. At the very least, this provides us with another avenue to become more aware and accepting in each moment, which as we have already discussed can reduce our levels of stress and increase our productivity and wellbeing. However, communicating like this offers much more. It offers the possibility of truly connecting with others, of improving relationships, increasing our understanding and being better understood. Ultimately, it provides an opportunity to recognise the interconnectedness between ourselves and others, which in turn can support our mindfulness practice as we feel more a part of something larger than ourselves, and consequently more at peace internally.

Healthy relationships

Communicating mindfully immediately starts to transform relationships. This is important as, for most people, relationships tend to rate toward the top of our list of what makes for a meaningful and happy life. They are also one of the things that cause us the most stress when they are not going well.

Much has been written about relationships for millennia and it would be impossible to do this justice in this chapter, but what we will focus on are some of the ways in which mindfulness can help form healthier, deeper, more fulfilling and more resilient relationships. The particular aspects that will be explored are:

- projecting onto others
- empathy and compassion
- dealing with hurt
- bullying
- cooperation and teamwork
- connectedness.

Projecting onto others

One thing that makes relationships most difficult is the tendency to go over and over old hurts, amplifying and reinforcing them. We can have arguments with people who aren't even there, hold onto stories about what happened long ago and project a whole lot of attitudes and assumptions onto others in terms of what we believe they are thinking. More often than not, what we take to be the reality of a situation has very little to do with the actual reality. This is not a good basis for healthy relationships.

Mindfulness helps us to see how much projecting we do. It's as if we walk around projecting a movie onto what is actually happening, and we confuse the two. This makes it very hard to respond appropriately to what is actually going on and, of course, if we take the movie to be real we have plenty of potential to get stressed and influenced by it.

Once we start to see clearly that this is going on, we can also start to see that this tendency doesn't get us anything good. Acknowledging this, we can then start to practise a new way of relating. We can let go of the attachment to the thoughts and feelings generated by all this mental projection. The unpleasant thought or feeling may recur, but it is the attachment to it that matters as far as whether or not we are influenced by it. Then, if we're standing back from the mental projection, we have the opportunity to stop identifying with projections, and start actually relating to the person in front of us. For example, we can reserve judgment about what the other person thinks, or not assume we know what they meant before we have the opportunity to ask them. And if we ask them, then it is better to ask in a mindful, inquiring, non-aggressive and non-defensive way.

Empathy and compassion

Once we start relating in this way, empathy and compassion tend to show up spontaneously. When we truly connect with another person (or animal, for that matter) we become attuned to their experience. We feel their joys as well as their sorrows. Spontaneous compassion then tends to arise as we recognise that they want to be happy just as we do, and that their suffering results from identifying with their judgments and limitations. We can relate to what the other is feeling because we have experienced similar kinds of experiences ourselves, even if we have not been in exactly the same situation.

Research shows that when we are present to someone's suffering, 'mirror neurons' and an area of the brain called the insula become active in our own brains and we feel their emotions as if they are our own.[1] It can be easy to become overwhelmed with this vicarious stress, and we can find ourselves telling the person to 'get over it' or can even avoid them altogether. This reflects our own difficulty in sitting with discomfort and tends to be a reaction rather than a useful response to their discomfort.

Remaining mindfully present to another's pain increases our own emotional intelligence and empathy.[2] Being at ease doesn't mean not caring or not helping if we can, it just means being less stressed by, or resistant to, the situation in front of us.[3] Interestingly, studies show that when we mindfully feel compassion, the empathy area in our limbic system becomes active, while the stress regions remain inactive. This could be very important in preventing 'carer fatigue', as it is sometimes called.

One challenge is that sometimes we are aware that we are about to be unkind to another person, and we might even notice the discomfort that comes with that, but we do it anyway. If we do that, then pretty soon we will have the opportunity to be mindful of the consequences that come with being unkind. Then we can decide whether or not being unkind really helps us to be at peace with ourselves. A good indication of the residual effect of being unmindful and unkind is the lack of mental peace and ease that follows as the mind endlessly talks to itself trying to justify something that may not have been just. It is important to remember that mindfulness is not about doing things 'perfectly' all the time, but is about being aware of the full gamut of our mental habits and learning from our experiences — both 'successes' and 'failures'.

Dealing with hurt

Sometimes it is us on the receiving end of injustice or unkindness. Again, we have a choice: do we hold onto the hurt and resentment, or do we accept and forgive? It is important to remember that acceptance is not the same as resignation, and practising mindfulness does not mean letting people walk all over us. But we can notice the effect of not forgiving and see whether that costs us more than to forgive. There tends to be nobody we hurt more with bitterness than ourselves, and the more we reinforce it, the more we will have to live with it in the future. At least if we are mindful we can make it more of a conscious choice whether or not to forgive and move on. If we do forgive and move on then we may notice not only a release in tension but also insight into why the person may have treated others poorly. Although it may not justify it, it does help us to understand. Forgiving others begins with forgiving ourselves, and we first need to practise bringing acceptance and love to ourselves before we can truly start bringing it to others.

Bullying

Bullying has always been an unfortunate part of school and the workplace. Sometimes the bullying is real and intentional, sometimes it is unintentional or even just in our perception. When people are bullying others, although they might look strong and assertive on the outside, on the inside they tend to be as anxious and depressed as the people they are bullying. It is often driven by low self-esteem, which bullies attempt to compensate for by dominating others rather than generating self-acceptance. It is therefore no surprise that bullies are four times more likely than the general population to have depression and they are far more likely to have suicidal thoughts, psychosomatic symptoms and a lack of warmth and connectedness at home.[4]

Bullying has become more of a problem today because of cyber-bullying and the use of social networking, where people can bully far more anonymously, venomously and widely. Before we say something unkind to another, two good tests of whether or not to do it are: first, to consider whether we would like others to treat us that way; and, second, to consider whether we would be happy to be seen doing it publically rather than anonymously.

If we are ever being bullied then it will help to speak to someone about it and have the situation dealt with rather than to suffer in silence.

Cooperation and teamwork

An important aspect of relationships in education and our personal life relates to cooperation and teamwork. We are social creatures and we can do more with each other's help than we can do by ourselves. Mindfulness helps the individuals of a team to work well collectively. Many learning activities in school and university involve students working together. Mindfulness can help us communicate more effectively, empathise more, be patient with each other when things don't go well and stay focused under pressure. It can help us be more aware of our thinking biases and expectations, and to manage ourselves better so we can operate effectively as team members. It is perhaps no surprise that a number of elite sporting teams are now using mindfulness to help improve cohesion, teamwork and performance.

Connectedness

Social isolation is associated with poorer mental and physical health. Connectedness, on the other hand, has the opposite effect. A massive study of the relationship between connectedness and adolescent health found that parent–family connectedness, perceived school connectedness and parents having expectations for higher standards of behaviour rather than not caring, were protective against health risk behaviours.[5] Also protective was having a spiritual or religious dimension to a person's life. If we want to do more to improve wellbeing among young people then we need to emphasise the importance of diminishing risk factors and promoting protective factors like connectedness.

•

Day by day, mindfulness practice will help us to be more at ease with ourselves and this helps us to be more at ease in whatever social situation we find ourselves, as well as being able to build better communication and social skills.

CHAPTER 12

eMindfulness

How paying attention helps us use media more wisely

In discussing communication we have touched upon the problems that can emerge when we post content online — placing it irreversibly in the public domain forever — without first taking a breath and considering what the implications might be. This is just one of the potential issues with the unmindful use of technology. Other problems include online bullying, disconnection from face-to-face social relationships, developing a passive learning style, and literally training ourselves to be inattentive and unfocused. In this chapter we explore these issues in more detail and look at ways mindfulness can help to address them.

We should start by saying that technology is neither good nor bad. It all depends on how it's used. Fire and language are both different types of technology and it should be pretty obvious that how these are used dictates whether they benefit or harm us as individuals or humankind in general. In the same way, new forms of technology and social media are tools that can be used to help or to harm. The key is in bringing awareness to how we use them.

Statistics show that around 90 per cent of families in developed countries currently have the internet at home, and this number is growing rapidly.[1] The internet is increasingly making the transition from being a portal for information and entertainment to being a setting in which people live their lives. It allows us unprecedented access to information, and allows us to share ideas instantaneously with a broad audience. We can use it to shop, study, share information and even seek medical advice. It is becoming more and more an integral part of life and is revolutionising society, generally in very positive ways. However, as we have already mentioned, there is also the potential for misuse.

Social media

While we can share inspiring information and keep people informed about our lives through posting information online, there is also the potential to exclude, harass and even bully people using social media. At its essence, online bullying is the same as more traditional forms, but technology means that many more people can be involved in the bullying and the effect can be far greater. Add to this the potential for photographs and video to be used to bully and harass people, and the potential for harm skyrockets. The illusion of anonymity contributes to this, as does the often passive, mindless use of technology. Jumping between tabs while simultaneously watching TV, for instance, literally trains inattentiveness, making it our default mode when using technology. Then, when we are posting information and ought to be paying attention to what we are doing and the potential consequences, we remain in this passive, consumerist trance and just hit 'send'. Mostly this doesn't create too many problems, but sometimes it does.

What we really need to practise is bringing more awareness to what we are doing and what the consequences may be. Simply taking a few mindful breaths before hitting send can save us a lot of problems later. Staying connected to our body — and therefore to our feelings — while writing email responses or online posts is also pretty useful. If we notice a strong emotion, we can pause and examine what is going on. When we are overwhelmed with emotions such as anger, anything we say or do is likely to further inflame the situation because in this state both our impulse control and rational thinking are not working too well. We are better off waiting until the feeling has passed and then responding to the situation, rather than reacting to the feeling (which tends to lead to attempts to get rid of the feeling rather than genuine efforts to resolve the situation in a meaningful, considered way). It is exactly the same with online communication. Sometimes just writing an angry email and then deleting it actually gives us the cathartic release we are looking for (or at least saving a draft and reviewing it a day or so later, once we have cooled down a bit). Better this than blindly hitting 'send'.

It is not just inattentive posting that causes issues, though. Research shows that if we start our day by answering emails, our productivity is reduced for the rest of the day. This is because checking emails first thing starts the day reactively, flooding our bodies with emotions that might have absolutely nothing to do with what we actually need to work on that day. It is far better to start the day by consciously planning what we need to do, and getting to emails later.

Another emerging problem with social media is the replacement of face-to-face social interaction with online communication. People who get their online versus face-to-face interaction out of balance are at risk of experiencing a range of problems, from a sense of isolation all the way through to full-blown depression.[2] Also, when communicating via texting and twittering we tend to communicate much more but with far less depth and meaning. Quantity has replaced quality. Our lives and minds have become cluttered with meaningless information. A US study on young people found that the amount of texting was inversely related to the amount of fulfilment within their intimate relationships.[3] While using technology can add much to our lives, it is also important to keep these issues in mind and balance online communication with face-to-face communication. A 20-second hug releases the hormone oxytocin in our brains, leading to a sense of calm and wellbeing.

Technology and a passive learning style

Technology can also encourage a passive learning style. Sometimes it's nice to tune out in front of the TV (or Facebook), but remember that what we practise gets literally hardwired into our brains, making it more and more likely that we will keep doing these things. When we practise things such as inattentiveness, we get better and better at doing *this*. Add to this a phenomenon called 'classical conditioning' — where we associate two separate events, for instance the sound of a bell with receiving food (in a classic experiment with dogs conducted by Ivan Pavlov) or going on a car trip with having car sickness — and we can start using *all* technology in an unmindful way. Then, when we get that email and react with a strong emotion, we have already written a response and hit 'reply all' before we have even really noticed what is going on.

It is important, therefore, to use technology in an intentionally more active and engaged way. A good start would be to use only one type of technology at any given time. As you may remember from Chapter 2, when we are being mindful we are activating parts of the prefrontal cortex that are associated with self-awareness and emotional intelligence. So when we post online mindfully we are strengthening the parts of our brain that lead to us being more aware, as well as associating the act of Facebooking with the quality of being self-aware.

Attention, screen time and brain development

Technology can work for and against us in other ways, too. Beginning in early childhood, both the type and the amount of media input have effects on executive functioning, the capacity to focus, and the risk of ADHD.[4,5] The more screen time a child has when young, the greater the risk of attention deficit problems later on. Why? A developing brain needs direct, sensory interaction with the environment to help it to establish and maintain neural pathways. Virtual experiences just don't do it. Attentional states and leisure activity are also associated with brain development and the rate of brain ageing. For example, older people who have greater participation in cognitively stimulating activities (particularly in early and middle life) have brains comparable to young people as indicated by reduced amyloid uptake (the protein that clogs the brain in Alzheimer's disease, or AD). Older people with the lowest levels of cognitively stimulating activity — for instance high amounts of screen time — have brain changes comparable to patients with AD.[6] Even more concerningly, people with more screen time throughout their adult years are nearly four times as likely to develop dementia.[7,8]

The other aspect of being a slave to technology is the stress that comes with being, or thinking we need to be, accessible 24/7 to the point that boundaries between home, school or work become so blurred they are no longer visible. Time away from technology is a luxury many believe they don't have now. For example, having the phone or computer by the bed and thinking that we need to check emails or send text messages in the middle of the night not only causes stress but it interferes with sleep, which leaves us more at risk of mental health problems.[9] Part of the stress is related to the 'tyranny of the urgent'. Things are perceived as being urgent even when they're not. And, increasingly, our devices are being designed to perpetuate this, for instance pop-up alerts on home screens.

Perhaps even more worryingly, an increasing number of us are addicted. For example, some studies report that up to 25 per cent of young people are addicted to their mobile phones, demonstrating qualities identical to any other kind of addiction, such as tolerance, withdrawal symptoms, inability to modify behaviour and impaired relationships with peers.[10,11]

Using technology wisely

To summarise this chapter, technology is neither inherently good nor bad. In addition, there is no right or wrong way to use it. But if we start paying attention to our experience while doing so, we may start to notice certain tendencies and certain associated effects. We may notice that at times we use it unmindfully and reactively, and that this is a habit we train ourselves to engage in. We might also notice that at times this causes problems for us, ranging from sending emails without attachments all the way up to creating Emailgate situations by replying with aggressive responses or releasing information into the public domain that with more awareness we would have kept private. When we act with enough unawareness we can even cause emotional distress for others via unintentional (or intentional) actions such as cyber-bullying, which would be much more difficult to do if the parts of our prefrontal cortex associated with self-awareness and compassion were activated in that moment.

Instead, try the following:

- Next time you use technology, experiment with using one platform/media type at a time, and observe the effects of this.
- Before sending emails or posting anything online, take a few mindful breaths and even check in with yourself in the ways outlined in Chapter 11.
- Be curious about which part of yourself wrote the email: whether it was a deeper, wiser part of you or perhaps just the storm of emotions or default mode reactivity on the surface.

CHAPTER 13
Enhancing creativity

It is not uncommon for people to ask whether mindfulness impedes creativity. The reasoning goes that the wandering mind is also the creative mind, and if it is not allowed to wander because we are focused on the here and now by tethering it to the senses, we might be suppressing our ability to be creative or imaginative. Perhaps, however, the truth is that the mindful mind is *also* the creative mind.

Creativity is as natural for human beings as breathing. Creativity and play go hand in hand. The younger we are the more creative our play will be. We draw, sing, write, act, solve problems and make things. Unfortunately, many of us lose the time or forget the fun of being creative and replace it with just surviving the demands of day-to-day life. So, how can mindfulness help us to do it better and rediscover the enjoyment that is naturally a part of creativity?

The mind is creative, but what is it creating?

When we sit to practise meditation, or when we watch the mind as we go about our day-to-day life, we will notice that the mind is innately creative.

It can't help itself. This can be a great blessing but it can be a curse if we are not using the mind's creative capacities consciously and skillfully.

Take anxiety about an upcoming exam, assignment or presentation as an example. The mind is most certainly being creative — creating worries, anticipation, catastrophes, dramas, sagas and all the rest. All this is happening in the imagination. What we do need to do — prepare for the event — is not getting any attention at all. What has gone wrong? The mind is running unchecked from one imagining to another while the capacity to discern between imagination and reality is not switched on. Thus we take imagination to be real and we fight with the phantoms it creates. This is the mind's imaginative capacity being misused. The mind, rather than being a faithful servant, has become a tyrannical master.

The mind's capacity to imagine is valuable and useful if we use it mindfully. This means using it in a way that is intentional and purposeful, where we retain the capacity to distinguish between imagination and reality, and can switch to another focus when we need to. Conversely, unmindful imagination is unintentional and purposeless; we lose the capacity to discern what is real from what isn't, and we get stuck in that mode even when it causes grief and wastes time.

Unmindful imagination vs vision and insight

There are three classes of people: those who see, those who see when they are shown, those who do not see.

Leonardo da Vinci

Do we always have to be focused on the senses to be mindful? Not necessarily. If the mind is imagining rather than being focused on the senses, this does not mean we are unmindful — we are just aware of the mind being creative. We could choose to give attention to the creative imagination or anything else we wish. While much of this book has focused on the ways we can use sensory awareness to remain present, we can also practise being mindful of thinking. Bringing an intentional, present-moment awareness to our thoughts, we can observe them arise from, play around in, and dissolve back into awareness. We can objectively observe thoughts coming and going like clouds in the sky, although it is easier to get lost in thoughts this way compared to keeping the attention on the body and senses. For this reason, mindfulness of thoughts is often taught later on in mindfulness courses, after participants have learnt to focus on the senses and cultivate an ability to stand back from, or be unattached to, the thinking process.

The more mindful we become, the greater our capacity to be less impacted upon by unhelpful imaginings and mental chatter. This leaves the mind a little clearer and more able to work effectively (i.e. being 'clear-headed', 'open-minded' or being 'lucid'). What we call 'thinking' is mostly mental clutter and it obscures or crowds out vision and insight.

Vision, in the sense of someone being 'visionary', really means a person being able to see something that has potential which needs to manifest, or will come into manifestation. It entails a depth of perception in association with perspective. Insight and intuition carry a very similar meaning.

The lucid moment of vision or insight has a different quality about it to the distracted and rambling mind that is wandering aimlessly through a forest of thoughts and worries. For a start, the lucid moment has a real sense of presence, brightness and awareness to it. The classic representation of this in cartoons is the 'light bulb' above the head. At those moments the mind stops, we feel connected and there is enjoyment. The light bulb is the moment of inspiration which can then unfold in detail. This is how Mozart described it in one of the letters attributed to him:

When I am, as it were, completely myself, entirely alone, and of good cheer — say, travelling in a carriage, or walking after a good meal, or during the night when I cannot sleep; it is on such occasions that my ideas flow best and most abundantly. Whence and how they come, I know not; nor can I force them. Those ideas that please me I retain in memory, and am accustomed, as I have been told, to hum them to myself. If I continue in this way, it soon occurs to me how I may turn this or that morsel to account, so as to make a good dish of it, that is to say, agreeably to the rules of counterpoint, to the peculiarities of the various instruments, etc. All of this fires my soul, and, provided I am not disturbed, my subject enlarges itself, becomes methodised and defined, and the whole, though it be long, stands almost complete and finished in my mind, so that I can survey it, like a fine picture or a beautiful statue, at a glance. Nor do I hear in my imagination the parts successively, but I hear them, as it were, all at once. What a delight this is I cannot tell!

It takes a clear and present, discerning mind in order to work in such a way and to be able to sift real inspiration and insight from the mundane thoughts that often pollute and crowd the mind. What can we do to help those light-bulb moments to come? Here are a few tips.

- Begin the creative process by practising some mindfulness meditation.
- Next gently rest the attention on the topic you wish to address.
- Avoid forcing the process.
- Be patient, open and settled, simply letting the stream of thoughts related to the topic come and go as they will.
- Keep coming back to this place of openness and presence any time you notice the attention has wandered off.
- Remain patient and wait until an idea comes along that has a spark of inspiration or insight about it.
- Follow that idea and see where it leads.
- If it leads nowhere useful, patiently come back to resting the attention again on the question, topic or medium.

Much of the challenge is resisting the temptation to make a poor idea into something it's not — a good one. We do this because we are impatient, don't trust ourselves or are afraid that nothing better will come along. Inspiration, however, rarely comes from anxiety. Put another way, the main trick to being on the platform for the right train when it comes along is not having already gotten on the wrong one because we got tired of waiting.

Translating vision into reality

One of the first challenges when we have a flash of inspiration is to not miss the moment. If we have the opportunity, follow the idea right there and then. Sometimes, though, we may not have time right at that moment to develop the idea, but it is useful to take the first reasonable opportunity that presents itself. Quite often, if we procrastinate or leave it for a few days, the brightness and spontaneity will have gone.

The next challenge is not to interfere with the creative process as it is unfolding. There are three main forms of interference.

First, we can get impatient and try to push the mind to work rather than let it flow. If we feel hurried it not only works less well but we also take the enjoyment out of the creative process.

The second problem is when we over-think or over-plan a creative idea as this disrupts the spontaneity of the process. We can become perfectionistic and agonise over how it is going to turn out to the point that, again, we lose the flow. So-called 'helicopter parents' can aggravate such a problem by constantly looking over their child's shoulder, creating anxiety about making a mistake and the negative consequences of mistakes.[1] Paradoxically, anxiety about making a mistake increases errors and reduces performance. In such a situation the attention is shifted from the task to the worry about the outcome of the task — that is, out of the present and into the future.

The third main problem interfering with creativity is distraction. Much has already been said about this and the remedy for it. Suffice to say here that distraction shows a lack of engagement and absorption in the creative process.

From a mindfulness perspective, it is much better to cultivate the capacity to sit back and let the mind work — to watch it work — rather than try to push it to work. Strangely, the more we feel as if we are 'doing' it, the harder it becomes; and the more we are watching the mind do what it does naturally, the easier it becomes. This does not mean that every idea the mind comes up with is necessarily of equal quality. Being mindful also means retaining the capacity to filter more useful ideas from less useful ideas and to make discerning choices regarding what to focus our attention on. If we get stuck, however, it is generally better to just keep moving, using the best of what comes to us even if we feel the idea is not inspired. This will help us to get back into the flow rather than become overly frustrated about a lack of progress. As one of the most creative minds of all time, Leonardo da Vinci, noted: 'Iron rusts from disuse; stagnant water loses its purity and in cold weather becomes frozen; even so does inaction sap the vigour of the mind.'

But if we really are only coming up with creative ideas of poor quality, then rather than waste time it might be better to go on with something else. It might be good to take a walk or read something of interest and then come back to the task when our mind is a bit clearer. When the creative process is flowing it comes with enjoyment, confidence and a sense of mastery.

Connectedness

One of the hallmarks of deep learners is seeing the connectedness between things — for example, how things being learnt in one subject relate to things learnt in another. Mindfulness makes it easier to see the connections between things that we may not have previously thought of as connected. It's the connectedness between things that makes them interesting and understandable. As Barry Commoner, the great environmentalist, said: 'The first law of ecology is that everything is related to everything else.'

Once connections between things start to become apparent, an infinite number of possibilities open up. For example, a medical student can struggle to learn about the complexity of human psychology, and the complexity of the immune system, and the complexity of the brain, and the complexity of genetics, but may never be taught that what goes on in our minds has direct effects on how our immune system works (for instance, the way exam stress increases the risk of coming down with infections), how our brain wires itself (neuroplasticity) and how our DNA expresses and repairs itself. Teaching details without perspective and interconnectedness is like giving information without understanding. It's dry and, like eating a packet of crispbreads, hard to take in.

All too often we are taught in such a way that puts knowledge into silos as if the universe was made up of things totally independent from each other. This is the exact opposite of how the universe actually is. As a result, we will often learn out of context and find it hard to see the relevance of what we are learning. This also makes learning a lot less interesting, and where there is no interest there will be little or no learning — and what learning does take place will require great effort. Fascination naturally draws attention, and where the attention goes insight naturally follows. An uninterested teacher will transmit that attitude directly to the students.

Mental flexibility and problem solving

Mental flexibility was discussed in Chapter 7 and just a few extra comments will be made here in the context of creativity. There is an important distinction between determination and perseverance, valuable character traits that will help us to learn, and mental rigidity, which will slow down and constrain learning. Getting fixed on an idea and unable to unhook from it interferes with flow and creativity. For example, we might be taking a very narrow view about there being only one way to write an essay, or one way to solve a problem. It's a mental rut that stops us from exploring new territory, improvising, trying new things and learning.

> *Insanity: doing the same thing over and over again and expecting different results.*
>
> Albert Einstein

Even if a creative idea doesn't work out that well, we should pay attention to this experience as it will help us learn and hone our ability to discern between creative ideas that are of higher quality and those that aren't. To quote Einstein again (someone who knew a thing or two about creativity): 'A person who never made a mistake never tried anything new.'

Mindfulness is all about our ability to stand back from the mind and its thoughts without attachment to them. If we can do that well, it helps us to view those ideas with greater impartiality and to let them go when they are not so helpful, and to be open to new possibilities.

Creativity from stillness

> *Those who have not found their true wealth, which is the radiant joy of Being and the deep, unshakeable peace that comes with it, are beggars, even if they have great material wealth ... The moment you start watching the thinker, a higher level of consciousness becomes activated. You then begin to realise that there is a vast realm of intelligence beyond thought, that thought is only a tiny aspect of that intelligence. You also realise that all things that truly matter — beauty, love, creativity, joy, inner peace — arise from beyond the mind. You begin to awaken.*
>
> Eckhart Tolle, *The Power of Now*

Lastly, we come to one of the more challenging and paradoxical aspects of the role of mindfulness in creativity — stillness. Creativity necessarily involves movement, but to begin the creative process it helps to start from stillness: in other words, to centre oneself before commencing. In stillness we can find peace, openness and the ability to stand back from the mind. Stillness only comes from non-attachment to all that is moving, such as the mind, emotions and senses. It connects us with the quiet intelligence beneath the thinking mind — this is where our creativity really springs from. It is for this reason that it is a very useful practice to put moments of stillness between the completion of one activity and the commencement of another.

CHAPTER 14

Movement and sport

Many people will note that after exercise they feel more clear-minded, alert, calm, energised and focused. The physical activity of exercising in itself has a whole range of physical and psychological benefits that are too long to enumerate here, but it is not just the physical activity that is important, it is also the state of mind we tend to cultivate when we exercise. This is a time when we tend to be more in the moment and engaged with what is happening. Exercise is generally a time when we are mindful and we take some of that with us after the activity. This is why it is good to exercise regularly, especially during demanding periods such as the lead-up to exams. We will feel better physically and mentally, and will study better. The evidence consistently confirms that students who exercise regularly compared to those who don't have better mental health, self-esteem and achieve better grades.[1,2]

Moving with attention

One of the ways to take mindfulness 'off the meditation cushion', so to speak, is to bring awareness to movement, making it a moving form of meditation. This is called 'kinesthetic awareness'. There are simple mindful movement practices such as mindful walking and stretching that are a great way of exploring this, as well as martial arts such as Systema, tai chi and aikido, which emphasise presence and awareness. However, mindfulness can be brought to every single movement you make and to every activity you engage in, from walking to the train station to washing the dishes, to studying, or even just turning on light switches. Mindful movement is a very effective way of embedding mindfulness in your daily life. It also affords us the opportunity to increase our efficiency of movement, reduces injuries and helps us perform better on the sporting field and in the classroom.

Turn to Exercise 6a, 'Mindful walking' (p. 221) and Exercise 6b, 'Mindful stretching' (p. 223) to help you bring mindfulness to your movement.

So what does it mean to move mindfully? As we pay increased attention to how we move and to the actual sensation of each action, we begin to move with greater precision, fluency and efficiency. Of course, most movements we make are largely automatic and do not require much conscious control. Take walking, for example. If you are like most people, somewhere around one year of age, give or take a few months, you started learning to walk. You had been crawling for a while and developing both dynamic coordination and muscle strength. Then, one day, you took hold of a piece of furniture and stood up straight. After standing in this position for some time, perhaps sitting down again periodically to feel the solidity and support of the ground once again, you took a first tentative step. Most likely you fell to the ground at this point, but with perseverance you learnt to stay upright for longer and longer periods and began to toddle around, moving from the realm of infancy into toddlerhood. Watch any child going through this learning process and you will see mindfulness in action. It generally takes all their focus to stay upright. Over time, with repetition and sustained practice, it becomes easier to stay upright for longer periods and begin to walk. This is helped along by the fact that the human brain during this period is set up for maximum plasticity, forming new neural connections and pathways effortlessly. Fast-forward a few decades and here you are, walking without paying it any attention at all until you suddenly step out onto some ice or some other unpredictable surface, and bam! You're completely aware of the act of walking once again.

Once learnt, walking, like most things, can be done quite effectively and automatically, and does not really require us to be mindful as we do it. It has become a simple task so that we can safely and effectively perform simple multitasking. However, as already mentioned, we can use mindfulness of walking to increase our general levels of awareness. There may also be times when we need to develop our awareness of it to increase our sporting performance. For instance, let's imagine the situation that many athletes face as they move from amateur to more elite levels. All athletes have their own individual ways of moving and playing, as each of their bodies is unique. However, it is an unavoidable fact that some ways of moving are more efficient than others.

In order to draw more attention to a physical activity as an exercise in mindfulness you can slow things *right* down. Things such as walking, that are so automated we can do them without thinking about them at all, are basically reflexes. If we keep doing them at full speed, we just keep repeating the same reflex. So the first step (excuse the pun) is to slow things down. This allows us to focus our attention more intensely on the particular movement we are seeking to change (we are using the example of walking but this applies equally to any movement from how we hold a tennis racquet to how we play a musical instrument). Slowing a movement down recreates the initial learning environment, so we are basically twelve months old again and learning how to walk.

Those who have seen the movie *The Karate Kid* will remember 'wax on, wax off'. This, by the way, is why martial arts such as Systema and tai chi are done slowly. There are certain instinctive reflexes, such as grabbing hold of someone's hands when they grab you, that are actually not all that effective when you are trying to defend yourself against an aggressor. For instance, it is much better to recognise that when somebody grabs hold of you they restrict their own options; then you can keep your own hands free and respond in a way that is more effective than just getting into a wrestling match. But such a response needs to be trained slowly and deliberately, or else we will fall back into old reflexive patterns and grab their hands as soon as they take hold of us.

To return to the example of the runner, once they stop they can begin to explore what is actually going on in that moment, beneath any reflexes or ideas they may have. Simply standing and feeling the body — the weight distribution, breathing and muscular activation, for instance — can be highly instructive. It becomes possible to notice where the tension is in the body (we *all* hold tension in our bodies, largely unconsciously) and thus to let it go. Perhaps we are leaning a little to one side — intentionally leaning from side to side and then finding our centre once again will help us explore this. Perhaps we are restricting our breath as we stand in this way, and simply letting go of tension somewhere in the torso or altering our posture will allow the breath to resume effortlessly. Once we have tuned in to our body in this way, we can take a mindful step, just one at a time, really feeling the weight transfer into the other leg and foot, while the muscles in our legs activate and deactivate. Then we can feel our heel come off the ground, followed by the ball of the foot. We can experience our leg and foot move through the air, and then feel the heel make contact with the ground in front of us. Then we can feel our weight transfer back into that foot and leg, and then repeat the process with the other. Presto! We have just taken a mindful step, perhaps our first since we were twelve months old. If nothing else, if we want a cure for impatience this is it.

This is how athletes can retrain inefficient movements and improve their performance. It is as simple as slowing things down, bringing awareness to their movement, practising until the new way is natural, and then speeding the movement up again. Of course, mindfulness doesn't *have* to be done slowly — it just has to be done *mindfully*. So once we become able to move slowly with awareness we can start speeding back up, ultimately becoming able to move at full speed while staying completely relaxed and aware, giving rise to true efficiency of movement.

We should mention that this same process can be used to retrain mental reflexes such as fear reactions. A friend of ours tells a great story about a formative experience in the nets at cricket training in his early teens. Someone tossed a bouncer that hit him in the forehead, knocking him out cold, meaning that he had to go to the emergency department for an assessment. The next time he found himself facing a fast delivery in the nets, he reflexively tensed up and ducked the ball. Then for the next ball he tensed up again and chipped it away ineffectively with the bat. Rather than the fear going away, it actually got worse with each delivery. Perhaps you can relate to this from your own experience, on or off the sporting field. What our friend (who, perhaps not coincidentally, later became a martial arts teacher) realised was that he needed to retrain this fear response into something more effective. So he did something very wise — he asked the bowler to use a tennis ball for a bit, and to slow the deliveries right down. Then he made sure he stayed relaxed and kept breathing throughout the delivery, and drew upon his previously acquired repertoire of movements to hit the ball effectively. Then, once his confidence increased and the fear reaction stopped showing up, he progressed back to using a hard ball and gradually got his teammate to increase the rate of the deliveries. Eventually he found he could face full-speed deliveries from bowlers from opposing teams intent on psyching him out, and stay completely relaxed, which he says is an improvement on how he was prior to the ball-in-the-face incident. He didn't just get back to his previous standard, he exceeded it because he was far more mindful now. This is an example of how mindful movement is not just for changing bad habits but can also be useful for anyone wanting to improve their performance in any sport.

The zone or flow state

A surprising number of elite athletes train their minds these days as much as they train their bodies. Take Phil Jackson, the legendary coach of the LA Lakers and Chicago Bulls, who took his teams to an unprecedented eleven NBA titles. Jackson's protégés, such as Michael Jordan, learnt the secrets of meditation and attention, enabling them to make far better use of their natural talents. When performing at our peak, in sport or any other endeavour, we are in a mindful state of a very high order. Billie Jean King, one of the greatest tennis players of all time, described the zone as follows:

> *It almost seems as though I'm able to transport myself beyond the turmoil on the court to some place of total peace and calm … I appreciate what my opponent is doing in a detached abstract way. Like an observer in the next room … It is a perfect combination of [intense] action taking place in an atmosphere of total tranquillity.*[3]

Many athletes later come to describe such experiences as spiritual. If you recollect peak experiences in your own life then these tips will make a lot more sense. The zone, or flow state, is basically the same state no matter what sport or activity it arises in.[4] Mihály Csíkszentmihályi noted some of its essential characteristics:[5,6]

Deep but effortless concentration on the process

The concentration is fully drawn by engagement and interest in the activity itself and not to some secondary goal, such as winning. Therefore these experiences are the most alive, vivid, fulfilling and memorable. This also implies an ability not to be interested in anything irrelevant, including being heckled by opponents.

A sense of self-control

The zone is a unified and integrated state. If there is no internal battle then there is nothing to pull us off balance or fight against because it's a state of non-attachment. There may be a hurricane of activity going on around us but we are in the 'eye of the hurricane' — some call it being centred.

An absence of self-consciousness or ego

When we are thinking about ourselves we are not on task, and when we are on task we are not thinking about ourselves. Although we are not self-conscious, the zone is the most self-expressive state.

Enjoyment, relaxation, confidence and freedom

What satisfaction there is when watching it happen with such effortlessness. What freedom of expression! What is there to be anxious about?

Focused on the goal although not anxious about it

The zone is not an aimless state. We are able to set the course with clarity and unwavering resolve and yet not pin our happiness on the outcome. There is resilience because we are no longer focused on the things that sap resilience — such as self-doubt — and so losing holds no fear.

In the present moment

The focus on the present leaves no room for preoccupation or anxiety about the outcome and allows attention to engage fully to optimise performance.

The sense of time is altered

Although events may be moving fast, things seem to slow down (which is a sign of acute attention). Although a long time may have passed while engaged in the activity, it seems to be no time at all. Some describe the present moment as being timeless.

Peak performance

Enough said.

•

The zone or flow state sounds pretty good and most of us would live there if we could. For many of us our desire to be in the zone is about performing well and for others it's about fulfilment and enjoyment. For others, such as rock climbers, it's about life and death — that's one way to bring the mind into the joys of being present! Being in the zone is not something we can do, it is more a matter of learning not to think our way out of it with worry, self-doubt and distraction.

Mindful movement in everyday life

So far we have focused mainly on using mindfulness to improve sporting performance, but as we mentioned at the start of the chapter, mindful movement is also a way to bring mindfulness more fully into your everyday life. Some people like to set aside time each day for deliberate mindful movement practices such as mindful walking or stretching. Some people join yoga or good (i.e. 'mindful') Pilates classes. As you can imagine, doing 5 minutes of mindful walking means you are much more likely to spontaneously become aware of your walking at other times throughout the day, thus becoming more generally mindful.

We have included mindful walking and stretching practices in Exercises 6a and 6b (pp. 221 and 223). You might like to practise these before exercising to get you more fully into your body, to improve performance and avoid injuries. You might also like to practise them at other times too, simply to increase your body awareness and explore other tools for developing mindfulness in each moment of your life.

Mindful sport

As well as practising the exercises included in Exercises 6a and 6b, you might like to start using these principles generally when you are training and playing sport. Here are some tips for doing this effectively:

- Slow things down and bring increased awareness to your actions.
- Use minimal effort to move. Notice tension in the body and let it go (some regular body scan practice will help with this). Notice the tendency (which we all have) to use too much effort or force when we move. Try to use just enough — not too little, not too much. As you might expect, this is a dynamic process of moving and checking in, moving and checking in.
- Keep breathing. We tend to hold our breath when we are scared or concentrating hard, and this brings tension into the body and mind, making us less efficient. Just keep feeling the breath during exercise, and make sure you don't hold it unless required for the activity (e.g. target shooting and especially free diving!).
- Use these same principles to get rid of mental tension (e.g. fear responses). You might have heard the expression, 'Feel the fear and do it anyway'. This is good advice, but requires that you slow things down otherwise you will just be triggering reflexes. Do things *really* slowly until you feel comfortable and can stay relaxed without holding your breath. Then speed it up gradually until you get back to full speed (or even beyond!).
- Explore your limits. Respect that you have limits, both physically (e.g. your cardiovascular fitness or how far you can stretch in any particular direction) and mentally (e.g. how much discomfort you can handle). Learn to recognise these limits, stay there, bring mindfulness to them until you can accept them and release any excess tension around them, and then gradually explore going beyond them.

- Be like a child. Play and enjoy! Little kids learn so fast and well because they are *curious* about what they do. Have fun and bring curiosity to whatever you are doing. Notice how that changes the experience of doing it. Most people find that doing this helps them learn faster *and* makes it more fun as they do so.

CHAPTER 15

Teaching with attention

There are many things that get in the way of teaching (and parenting) mindfully. The less mindful the teacher (or parent), the greater the chance of having less mindful students. The major barriers to teaching mindfully include the following:

Attention deficit trait (ADT). Studies in the workplace have shown that in the 'hyperkinetic' (time-pressured, fast-paced) work environment workers tend to have shorter attention spans. ADT is associated with issues such as black and white thinking, difficulty staying organised, setting priorities and managing time, and a background level of panic and guilt.[1] Schools are classic examples of the hyperkinetic environment.

Burnout. Burnout has three aspects — depersonalisation, lack of personal accomplishment, and emotional exhaustion. In burnout we care a lot less about our work and those for whom we are working.

Stress and poor mental health. When we do not feel well mentally and emotionally we tend to spend a lot of time in default mode, and performance and executive functioning suffer as a result. Furthermore, stress is a 'communicable disease' in that we tend to pass it on to those around us.

Blurred boundaries between work and personal life. When we take home with us a mental preoccupation about work, or take a preoccupation about home to work, we lose focus on what we are doing. Being able to switch from home to work and be present at each matters enormously for wellbeing, enjoyment and performance.

Multitasking. When we are time-pressured we tend to try to compensate by multitasking, which only adds to the problem, reduces efficiency and increases errors and stress. If teachers and parents do this in front of children then it is being unconsciously taught to them by example.

Automatic pilot. When suffering from 'presenteeism' (just presenting to work without really engaging with it), we deliver a far poorer service and don't respond nearly as well to our environment and the people in it.[2]

Over-reliance on screen media. Attention, especially for a young and developing brain, engages far less well for screen-based media than with a more tactile, 'real' experience. Studies consistently show that the greater the screen time for children and adolescents, the greater the chance of attention deficit problems.[3,4] On average, children in developed countries have 4 to 5 hours of screen time daily, which is well over the maximum safe limit of 2 hours a day recommended by most authorities. Possibly a quarter of children are now addicted to electronic media and communication devices.[5]

Complacency. When we feel complacent or have taught the same thing a number of times we tend to do it on automatic pilot. We may be doing a competent job but we are functioning habitually without necessarily engaging our attention let alone the students'. Spontaneity, creativity, self-improvement and innovation don't happen when we are complacent, as they are traits of the mindful teacher.

Cultivating mindfulness

So the question is, how do we cultivate mindfulness within the teaching environment for the benefit of students and ourselves? Outlined below are some tips and strategies.

Creating a mindful environment

An environment can be either conducive or hostile to fostering mindfulness. One of the best ways to assess this is to quietly sit back and notice what the quality of attention is like in the room. Also looking at the room while it is empty of students is useful: clutter, untidiness, disarray and overcrowding, for example, tend not to help.

Managing inputs and distractions. It's easy to get swept along in the busyness and pace of a school or home environment but it is important to be in charge of it rather than dominated by it. For example, when three people come up at once demanding attention it is wise to take them one at a time while asking the others to wait. It might be possible to cut down on unnecessary noise and close down non-essential activities.

Managing media. It is fashionable to assume that being online opens up a larger world. It does offer a large volume of superficial experiences but this is a poor replacement for depth of experience associated with real interaction. Electronic media and screen time is not 'bad', it just needs to be used discerningly. A general rule for teaching could be to never teach something on screen that could be taught with real, tactile experience.

Self-care

Apart from taking time for regular mindfulness practice it is important to take time to care for our wellbeing in other ways. At Monash University we use the ESSENCE model, with essence being an acronym standing for Education, Stress management, Spirituality, Exercise, Nutrition, Connectedness and Environment. Taking time for self-care is not an exercise in self-indulgence, it's an investment in our ability to care for others in a sustainable way. Self-care helps to enhance mental health and avoid burnout. Work–life balance also matters. When committed to our job, or anxious about performance, it is easy to overwork, but it is better to take time to look after ourselves and then feel fresh and alert when we work than to just pump out work hours with diminishing levels of interest, enjoyment and efficiency.

Teaching style

The way we teach can help or hinder mindfulness. Consider the following issues.

Helicopter teachers

Although teachers (and parents) being interested and encouraging is associated with better outcomes, studies suggest that constantly hovering over students and being over-controlling has negative outcomes for students emotionally and academically.[6,7,8] In mindfulness terms, this tendency reflects preoccupation, not attention.

Anxiety about performance

Creating an atmosphere of anxiety about outcomes slows down learning and directs attention from the learning task to self-consciousness. In the modern day of performance targets and school rankings this problem has become endemic among students, teaching staff, schools and parents.

Enthusiasm, fun and interest

Learning will happen most effortlessly and enjoyably where there is enjoyment because attention will naturally go where interest goes. The enthusiasm of the teacher will be infectious, as will the boredom and disinterest of the teacher. Fun or humour is a natural antidote to stress and will ease up the neural pathways to do what they need to do.

Modelling

Whether we are conscious of it or not, what we model at school will be taken up by students, especially the younger ones. Most of what we teach we actually do without awareness. This is why it is vital before a teacher even thinks of teaching mindfulness that they have applied it in their own life first and then take that into the classroom.

Pacing and variation

If we do things at the same pace all the time we can induce an automatic pilot state. Left, right, left, right … It is helpful to vary the pace and method of teaching; for example, something active and interactive followed by some time for discussion and then a little quiet or reflective time before moving onto the next activity. The whole class might be discussing a topic as one, followed by time for small-group interaction and then working alone. Without overdoing it, variety will help to maintain attention, especially for the modern young mind addicted to novelty.

Multitasking

Enough said!

Communication

It is easy to speak to students without attention, or not to really listen to them while they are speaking to us, especially if we are stressed, hurried, multitasking or disinterested. Speaking with attention is vital, especially if we want students to listen with attention.

Responding to the moment and spontaneity

The chance for spontaneity is negligible when on automatic pilot, teaching by rote, rigidly following a lesson plan or not being personally engaged with what is being taught. Spontaneous moments are the most creative and interesting ones and they are only to be found in the present moment and only by a flexible, engaged and responsive mind.

Encouraging openness

The openness to one's moment-by-moment experience practised in mindfulness meditation should be taken directly into the classroom. Encouraging students to speak openly about their experiences, challenges and questions helps learning enormously. Feeling that they can't speak openly means students pretend to understand when they don't, and don't ask questions when they need to. This happens a lot for children with fixed mindsets who are anxious to hide their inability to perform well. Open communication should not be confused with merely venting, particularly if doing so in a rude or disrespectful way.

Seeing the novelty in things

When we think we know something we tend to stop looking. Seeing the novelty or subtle distinctions in things is one of the favourite ways Harvard psychologist Ellen Langer emphasises for enhancing mindfulness, mental flexibility and performance and for reducing bias.[9,10] Sometimes when we 'over-learn' things we perform worse because we stop looking, learning, adapting and experiencing with depth.[11] We go on in life thinking we know things that we may not know at all or think that our limited range of experience is all there is to be experienced.

Don't take anything for granted

It is helpful not to take anything for granted because we never know, despite what we think, what the future holds. We also don't appreciate what we have if we take it for granted. The simplest things in life provide a multitude of simple pleasures if we care to notice them.

Mindfulness skills and experiments

There are lots of ways of bringing mindfulness more overtly into the classroom.

Using meditation: full stops and commas

It can be helpful to teach students longer (full stops) and shorter (commas) forms of the meditation practice to help punctuate the day. Obviously for younger children a couple of minutes is a long time so it is helpful not to overdo it. Starting and finishing a class with one or two minutes to assist students to settle, relax and focus will help, and a comma can also be useful when transitioning from one teaching activity to another within the class. There may be times in the day and the week when the class, or even the whole school, has a longer period of quiet. Using a gentle meditation bell or singing bowl can help to facilitate students moving into periods of formal mindfulness practice.

Experiments in mindfulness

Mindfulness is not just about meditation. Experiments such as mindful eating, mindfully listening to music, mindful communication, mindful drawing or being mindful while playing sport are all ways of enhancing the exploration and experience of mindfulness. These can be compared to doing similar tasks in habitual, non-mindful ways. You could ask students to perform some task such as comprehension or solving puzzles while multitasking and compare their performance to when they are not multitasking. If you're really adventurous you can do walking meditation. Such experiments only work well if children are engaged and quiet enough to notice the differences in experience, enjoyment, performance or how their minds and bodies work. A book and program by the name of *Meditation Capsules* is a good example of a range of mindfulness experiments aimed particularly at primary-aged children.[12] If you lead such practices then it is good to take some time for debriefing the activity afterwards.

Dealing with distracter influence

Distractions can be internal, in the form of thoughts and sensations, and external, mostly in the form of sounds. Students are often studying in environments where there is a lot of noise and potential distraction so particular attention can be given to helping students to deal with 'distracter influence'. One thing that will have probably already been noted is that trying to block out distractions only makes them more intrusive and the student more frustrated. This is because in trying to block something out we are actually focusing on it as we monitor the environment to see if the distraction is still there.

See Exercise 12, 'Working with distractions' (p. 237) for an experiment in dealing with distracter influence.

Building mindfulness into the curriculum

It helps a lot if mindfulness is not taught as a separate skill divorced from other aspects of the curriculum; it needs to be integrated with other content. For the medical students at Monash University the case for its inclusion in the core curriculum included:

- enhancing student wellbeing and building resilience
- enhancing study skills
- managing exam anxiety
- preventing carer burnout as doctors
- enhancing clinical performance, empathy and communication skills
- integrating biomedical, psychological and social sciences with clinical medicine
- laying foundations for future clinical skills in lifestyle and stress management
- fostering peer support
- fostering experiential and deep learning.

Within your school or university there might be a different list of priorities to make mindfulness relevant but it is really just a matter of finding what is important and emphasising the aspects or applications of mindfulness that fit. Personal or emotional development, study skills and coping with exam anxiety will be relevant to virtually everyone whether in the classroom or on the sporting field.

Mindfulness can be even more deeply integrated into the curriculum. For example, a six-week program in mindfulness for 'wellbeing' or 'academic success' can be taught at the same time in semester as the students are studying biology.

The biology teacher can incorporate the science of mindfulness with learning about basic physiology and the human brain. This can be enhanced with experiments in class on attentional blink, comprehension and memory tasks with and without multitasking, or comparing outcomes before and after mindfulness practice.

Students can measure blood pressure or heart rate variability with and without mindfulness while they are learning about the relaxation and fight or flight responses.

They can test their capacity to solve problems or performance on hand–eye coordination tasks at the start of the six-week program and compare it at the end.

Students can be encouraged to be more aware of their own emotions and reactions as they learn about the brain and which parts govern which aspects of behaviour.

There is the potential for 'mindfulness fatigue' if the students have mindfulness classes year on year and they feel they are covering the same ground rather than looking at what it means to be mindful in new and innovative ways. Different variations on practices along with new resources can reinforce the sense that the students are building on a skill rather than repeating one. Therefore it helps to grade and build tasks over years, for example:

Primary school

Years 1–3: simple mindfulness exercises to provide some quiet at the start and end of class.

Year 4: learning about the effect of worrying versus being calm.

Year 5: a range of mindfulness experiments for each of the five senses such as mindful eating, listening to music and observation.

Year 6: mindfulness and creativity experiments.

Secondary school

Year 7: mindfulness of communication and relationships including experiments in multitasking.

Year 8: mindfulness applied to sport, dramatic or artistic performance.

Year 9: the basics of mindfulness and human biology (see above).

Year 10: mindfulness and emotional regulation.

Year 11: mindfulness applied to enhancing academic performance.

Year 12: mindfulness in stress reduction.

Tertiary

Leadership, professional development, higher executive functioning and self-care.

Obviously there are many potential innovations and variations on the above theme, but the point is for the students to get the sense that mindfulness is the generic skill that underlies so many other skills and capacities and that development of it takes time and maturity.

CHAPTER 16

Working with resistance

It would be nice if every student, every teacher, every school, every person took to mindfulness like a duck to water, but it's not quite like that. It is not uncommon, and not necessarily wrong, to experience resistance to mindfulness. We can look on such a situation as either a problem or as an opportunity — we prefer the latter.

Mindfulness cannot be imposed on a student. They will need a level of motivation and insight in order to engage with the process. Otherwise they will just pretend to go through the motions to keep the teacher happy or, even worse, they will build up resistance and resentment to mindfulness — an attitude that might be difficult to shift.

Communicating to students, other staff and parents what mindfulness is and how it might be of benefit is extremely important. Nowhere is this more so than in educational institutions attempting to implement a 'whole school' approach to mindfulness, as is the case at Monash University and some of the secondary schools we consult to. The following suggestions are based on our years of experience communicating the message, working with resistance and making mindfulness relevant.

Imposing doesn't help

Mindfulness can only ever be offered; the choice is always the person's own as to whether they will take up the gift. If we look at the matter clearly enough, the need for mindfulness tends to be self-evident but we have to see it for ourselves — we cannot look through another's eyes. Imposing the practice runs the risk of galvanising resistance, not dissolving it.

Make mindfulness relevant

Working with resistance is generally an exercise in communicating the message better and making mindfulness relevant to that individual or group in terms that make sense to them. For example, a fifteen-year-old male might not be interested in inner peace but he might be interested to learn why elite footballers learn these skills. A postgraduate university student may or may not be interested in reducing stress, but they might be interested in the relationship between focus, verbal fluency and executive functioning as they try to write their thesis. It is a good idea to ask the individual or group what is important to them and then, as best as you are able, explore why mindfulness might be useful in that regard.

We also emphasise the everyday nature of mindfulness. We commonly start our programs and presentations by reflecting on experiences of being on automatic pilot and the problems associated with that. We also invite people to reflect on times in their lives when they naturally experience moments of mindfulness such as when exercising, eating their favourite food, playing with the family, watching a sunset at the beach and so on. This helps to demystify mindfulness and imparts the message that it is a state of being familiar to us all. We talk about these experiences as being 'accidental' moments of mindfulness and then explore how that quality of awareness can be cultivated and developed through practice. Going about it in this way ensures that mindfulness doesn't become seen as some esoteric exercise designed to achieve some 'Zen-like' state of being, but is a way of increasing these already familiar experiences of being fully awake and present.

It is good to ask participants what comes up for them in response to the word 'meditation'. Often people think of monks or mystical experiences, or that it is about 'getting rid of your thoughts'. Ask whether they have ever been able to fully and permanently get rid of their thoughts — nobody ever says yes. Mindfulness meditation can then be presented as a way of becoming grounded in the present moment, through attending to the senses, which is a way of not getting caught up in thinking, even though thoughts still appear. This normalises mind-wandering, debunks the myth of thought-stopping, and also gives people a way of staying centred even in the face of a barrage of thoughts.

Invite experimentation, questioning and inquiry

In learning about mindfulness it is helpful to establish an attitude of experimentation right at the outset. It's not a matter of having the right or wrong experience but rather having the experience we're having and learning from it. In that way, even if we attempt mindfulness meditation for the first time and find that the mind remains busy throughout, and then we try to get rid of the thoughts (which only results in the intrusiveness of those thoughts increasing), we have a great opportunity to note what this experiment is trying to teach us. Then we could experiment with an attitude of not judging the thoughts or even thinking that they are a problem and not being interested in them. Note the effect of this.

We do not understand much from the inside-out if we are just told what the lesson is. To learn the lesson for ourselves it helps to question and inquire, not tell. If resistance is present then being told to stop it, or that it is wrong, will tend to entrench the resistance whether or not the person continues to outwardly express it. From a perspective of teaching mindfulness, learning to ask questions is a very useful skill to develop because if we ask the right questions a person can then come to their own answers and conclusions with ownership over them. That way, mindful inquiry is a cooperative process, with teacher and student working together rather than against each other. At the beginning a student might think they are doing poorly when they were in fact sitting on a gold mine of valuable insights that just need to be drawn out. This education as 'drawing out' is what makes mindfulness such an effective means of self-discovery. In fact, one of the most powerful and transformative aspects of learning mindfulness — particularly in a group — is being able to remove labels of 'right' and 'wrong', 'good' and 'bad' from our experiences, so we can look directly at them with discernment rather than the usual reactivity that tends to close down any further exploration. Just telling a student what to think is not education (drawing out) but indoctrination (putting in).

Welcome whatever comes forth and work with it

If, as a participant in a mindfulness program, we feel that we are expected to give the 'right' answer to a question — for example, feeling expected to say that the meditation exercise was peaceful when it wasn't — we will either close down and not speak about our actual experience or we will concoct a 'nice' response to keep the teacher happy. Either way, we won't learn anything because we only learn when we explore and see things the way they are.

Mindfulness is best learnt and taught within an atmosphere of safety where we can say exactly what happened. It helps if we do that respectfully. Even if there are no mindful moments to report on, there may be unmindful ones which can be welcomed just as openly because they are equally instructive. A teacher can explicitly ask about these moments, and about any difficulties getting a routine of mindfulness meditation going, as this encourages the truthful and open expression of both successes and 'failures'. Seeing what gets in the way can be very revealing. At the same time, it is important that students speak in a group as much or as little as they are comfortable with.

There are no 'negative' or 'wrong' experiences, nor are there 'mistakes'. There is only experience. The question is whether or not we are learning from it. Indeed, there are pleasant and unpleasant experiences, and there are easy and difficult ones, and there are peaceful and unsettled ones, but from a learning perspective they are all equally valid and useful. If we explore we can learn the most important lessons from the most difficult experiences, which creates a kind of alchemy where lead, in the form of a difficult experience, is turned to gold, in the form of insight. The aim is to inquire into what happened with an open frame of mind and see what it shows us. If we learn from the experience then we are better off for having had it, even though it might have been unpleasant. If we don't learn from it then we are destined to keep repeating it until we do learn from it — Groundhog Day!

We work at our own pace

Resistance might be there for a reason. For example, a person might be so intimidated or disheartened by what they see going on in their minds that they try to avoid noticing it. Mindfulness, being all about awareness, will make it more obvious to us, but we might not feel ready to learn to work with it yet. The resistance to the practice of mindfulness is a kind of self-preservation. The fact that the problem is ultimately being preserved by not looking at it might not be evident to the person, but that barrier has to be respected and worked with before the person can progress safely and confidently of their own volition. For example, a person with significant anxiety who is forced to practise when they are unwilling to can experience rebound or heightened anxiety and might not have the openness of mind to welcome the experience and learn to work with it.

Valuing both formal and informal practice

It is helpful for a person to work with mindfulness in a way they feel comfortable with. They might do little formal practice because it makes their anxiety more obvious to them, but they might get a lot of value from the informal practice or cognitive aspects. Later they might feel ready to engage with the formal practice.

Some participants in mindfulness programs come back at the end of the week reporting very little if any formal meditation practice. It might be apathy, but it could also be concerns of the type just described. Either way, if the person feels like they will be criticised for not practising the meditation then they might pretend to be practising, or they might not speak, or not come back at all. Just looking at what gets in the way of practising meditation can be as interesting and instructive as looking at all the ways the habit-dominated mind has to avoid being mindful. There may be significant insights and benefit from the informal practice of being mindful in daily life. Welcome that and work with it. The formal practice could become more regular in the future, especially if that group member hears week by week what others in the group are discovering.

What the students say matters more than what the teacher says

The teacher is mainly there to foster inquiry and discovery. It is what the class members say that has far more authority for other class members than what the teacher tries to convince them of. Week by week, those who are practising and gaining insights will bring others in their wake. When a teacher is doing their job well they are more like conductors, drawing out the experiences of each participant, inviting others to reflect on their own experience in light of the insights that emerge from other group members, and generally being supportive of mindful inquiry. At its best it is an effortless process. During these moments, the level of presence, acceptance and humanity in the room can be palpable.

At least don't disturb others

If there is resistance to the point that a person doesn't want to engage in the process at all then that choice needs to be respected because we can't and shouldn't be forced into mindfulness. We can be encouraged or invited, but we can't be forced. In such a situation it is important that the person is quiet and respectful enough of the class in order not to disturb others. This includes not looking around the room during meditation practices, as this will tend to make others who are meditating nervous or self-conscious. Even being present in the class and hearing the reflections and insights of other class members will be enough to lead to a level of learning and interest although it may not be displayed.

CHAPTER 17

Managing personal stress in the classroom

As well as helping students reduce their stress, there will be times when educators need to manage their own. A number of factors lead to teacher burnout, including student discipline problems, being emotionally overwhelmed, and feeling disconnected from students and colleagues.[1,2] In this chapter, we look at how mindfulness can help address these issues so that teaching can remain fulfilling and rewarding.

To begin with, it is important to remember that stress is not inherent in the situation itself. Mindfulness shows us that it is stressful enough trying to control our own thoughts and emotions, let alone trying to control the thoughts, beliefs, moods and behaviours of a whole room of young people. But that is not to say that a teacher should just let the students do whatever they want and completely lose control of the classroom. Again, bringing it back to our own individual mindfulness practice, we can remember that acceptance is not the same as resignation. That is, accepting unpleasant thoughts and emotions when they occur is a good way to step out of the habitual struggle with them that adds an extra layer of stress to an already difficult situation. That said, we don't simply give in and let these unpleasant thoughts and emotions dominate and run us. Instead, we can learn to accept that they are there, observe them impartially (as best we can) and simply reorient our attention to what we need to be focusing on in that moment.

A useful — if perhaps somewhat strange — analogy to help illustrate this is buying a purple house. Imagine that you buy a new house on eBay. Perfect location, right number of bedrooms and so on. However, when you get there you find the house is bright purple. You can choose to freak out and start ranting to yourself, 'Damn it, who builds a purple house? I'm going to pull out of the deal! I can't believe they would do this to me! It's false advertising!' Now you are tense and angry — and still have a purple house. Or you could resign yourself to living in a purple house, and start thinking about the excuses you will make so you don't have to invite anybody over, and maybe go to the pharmacy to get some painkillers for when your resentment and anger gets too much and you get a headache. But there is a third option. You could *accept* that the house is bright purple: not at all the colour you would choose, but it is the colour that it *is*. And then you can take a breath, go to the hardware store and buy some paint and brushes, and get started repainting.

Similarly, someone doing one of our mindfulness courses recently said that he used to internally rant and rave about the volume of work he needed to do. When he practised being mindful he noticed the waste in ranting and raving. He then accepted the situation was the way it was and engaged his attention with the task, step by step. His stress went down and productivity went up! That's a win–win situation. It also illustrates the fact that acceptance and resignation are totally different things, and that to accept is not to give in completely and let something run (or ruin) your life. Acceptance is a necessary first step toward any change you want to make, because if you are reacting to something, you are too busy pushing against it to see the situation clearly and start doing whatever needs to be done to make the necessary changes.

In the same way, accepting what comes up in each moment in the classroom or lecture theatre is an important first step in creating meaningful change. Being grounded in your own body and present in each moment also helps to navigate the other challenges inherent in teaching, such as managing emotions, staying connected to others, and maintaining contact with your own values.

Maintaining discipline in the classroom

When we stay fully connected to what is happening in each moment of an exchange with another person, being attuned to more than just the words being said, we co-create an opportunity for true communication to occur. In the same way, maintaining effective discipline in a classroom begins with how we discipline ourselves. Here we can again use mindfulness as a laboratory for exploring through our experience how this actually takes place. Most of us tend to discipline ourselves by holding in mind a fixed idea of how we want things to be, and use a mixture of self-criticism and comparison to an ideal to keep moving in the directions we want to. However, in the moments we are doing this, our attention is in the future rather than being responsive to the present, and we create mental (and often physical) tension.

An alternative way to develop discipline starts to become apparent once we begin practising working mindfully with our experiences. Mindful discipline is all about generating the freedom to consciously choose what works best over what doesn't. Only a reactive and habitual and unconscious choice could ever be against our own best interests. Once we develop a little mental space between our experiences and that which is aware of them, we can start to make discerning choices about which thoughts and emotions we identify with or are going to serve us best. That is, if we see thoughts as just thoughts and experience two different thoughts moving through our mind in a particular moment — 'I want to sit and do a body scan for 5 minutes' and 'I want to watch TV' — we can simply choose not to identify with the thought about watching TV and instead focus on the thought about how much we want, or need, to meditate. What we focus our attention on soon becomes our reality, leading to speech and eventually behaviour.

Interpersonally, this same principle holds true. We all know that some bad behaviour is about getting attention. So, if we are able to simply not give it more attention than it deserves, by keeping our attention on something that does deserve attention, the attention-seeking behaviour often subsides all by itself. Of course, this becomes infinitely easier if we regularly practise mindfulness meditation, since part of the discipline of mindfulness is about redirecting our attention any time it gets lost in something we are not choosing to focus on in that moment. Simply not giving energy to bad behaviour in the classroom can be quite effective — and meanwhile we can focus our attention on what is important.

However, at times, we also need to set limits. In terms of our own individual practice, sometimes we work too hard, spend too much money and give too much so that we feel depleted or burnt out. In these situations it is actually appropriate to set some limits. This becomes easier to do as we develop the discernment and clarity that comes from being more in touch with each moment, rather than reacting habitually to what is happening.

In the classroom, the same rule applies. At times it is absolutely necessary to contain bad behaviour. But when this is done reactively it tends to lead to strong emotions and negative consequences for the relationship of the teacher with the student. When we instead take a breath, centre ourselves and get really present to what is happening in both the situation and our body and mind in response to it, we can start afresh and have more options. We can make a discerning choice as to how we respond, and can do so much more appropriately and effectively. It becomes possible to be very clear and definite, yet at the same time connected to our hearts and to the student in front of us. Compassion can at times mean being gentle and accepting, and at others look more wrathful, such as a parent scolding their child for running onto the road chasing a ball. It might look like anger but the emotion actually comes from a place of deep caring, as well as a clear perception of the situation.

'Heartfulness' is inseparable from mindfulness. But for the purposes of this chapter it is enough to say that just as being mindful doesn't mean *never* again thinking of the past or future, being heartful and caring doesn't mean never raising our voice or laying down the law when it really is required. What will tend to stop us from doing that will generally be attachment to an emotion such as fear or a thought such as 'What will everyone think of me?'. Letting go of such unhelpful attachments helps us to speak and act when we need to.

Managing our emotions in the classroom

Throughout this book we have explored how mindfulness can be used to very effectively manage stress and difficult emotions. We will not go into a great deal more detail here, but will offer some practical suggestions for using mindfulness to help navigate difficulties in the classroom.

The first and most obvious is stress. There is the stress of performing in front of a class, the stress of marking assignments, of deadlines, being assessed ourselves and so on. All of these, as we have discussed throughout the book, have to do with our mind habitually wandering off into worries about the future, regrets about the past, or judgments and reactions about the present. Obviously, the solution is to keep our attention in the present as much as possible. What is it that you are actually experiencing right now? What can you see in front of you? What sounds are coming to you right now? Even in the apparent din of a noisy classroom, can you make out individual sounds? Can you hear your own breathing as well as the sounds around you? Tuning in to your senses in this way gets you into the present and out of thoughts of past and future. This leads to clearer thinking, more effective communication and teaching and reduced levels of stress. Simply feeling your feet touching the ground, noticing the pressure and weight distribution, and feeling the support that the floor gives you as it holds you up against gravity — noticing all of this can be very helpful to literally ground you and stop you getting lost in stressful thoughts. Doing this, you can also start to notice your emotional state: tense, shallow breathing is a sign of mental tension and possibly frustration or even anger. Noticing this through the breath lets us catch it early, before we react. Another excellent centring exercise is to simply notice five things that you can see right now, and silently name these to yourself. Then notice five things you can hear, and finally five things that you can feel making contact with your body right now. This again gets you very quickly into your senses.

And even if you do find yourself caught up in the midst of an emotional reaction, it is possible to just sit with it by being willing to fully feel the sensations that come with it. It helps to breathe with the sensations and be really curious about them, as outlined in Exercise 8. Doing this helps you to not react to the emotions, and also keeps you as present as possible, meaning that you can make clearer, more discerning decisions regarding how to respond.

Turn to Exercise 8, 'Working mindfully with emotions' (p. 225), for practice in sitting with emotional experiences, rather than reacting to them. Remember that the key is to tune in to the body sensations and to be curious about how these actually feel, from moment to moment.

In Chapter 11 we explored ways of communicating more mindfully. When applied in the classroom, this can significantly reduce stress and improve connectedness. When we start communicating mindfully we tend to notice — often with a great deal of surprise — that we feel much more connected to people. This includes people we previously held a low opinion of or had conflict with. On this note, you may notice from the wording of the last sentence that we often hold opinions of others — both positive and negative — and this shapes how we experience the person, independent of what they are actually doing in any given moment. It leads to a kind of fixed mindset about people and relationships. If we expect someone to act in a particular way, we are more likely to perceive them doing so. Added to that, if we see ourselves as superior to others we are always in bad company! It is much better to use our capacity for discernment to notice the positive qualities in others and focus our attention on these rather than on shortcomings and flaws. It is one of the main laws of Positive Psychology that if we give all our attention to the negative then we feed it — and in our use-it-or-lose-it nervous systems, the positive dwindles through neglect.

Managing expectations

Another significant source of stress is expectations, both those placed on us by others and those we place on ourselves. Obviously we need to meet certain standards in our work, but it is important to find ways to respond mindfully to them, without taking them on in ways that cause us undue stress or difficulty. The first step is to see them for what they are: expectations. At their essence, expectations are ideas about the future and comparisons with how we are performing right now. We have already explored in detail how when our mind gets caught up in thoughts of the future we tend to experience stress, and that the more present we are, the clearer and more effective we tend to be. However, we have also made the point a number of times that mindfulness is not about *only* focusing on the present moment and never, from this day forth, having thoughts of the past or future again. When we are operating at our best we tend to be living mainly in the present yet are able to accurately recall the past and predict the future based on current trends. However, this conscious thinking of the past and future is very different to worry and regret. In fact, if we are really paying attention in the present we can predict the future better because we are seeing more clearly what is taking place and where it will lead.

Likewise, we need to be aware of what is expected of us, as well as what we hold to be important ourselves. There are deadlines that must be met if possible and certain minimum standards for our work, both organisational and personal. To achieve these we need to, at times, reflect on the past and future. We also need to be able to 'discerningly' observe our own behaviour. As we discussed in the last chapter, discernment means to see things clearly and notice the differences between them so that we can respond appropriately to situations. It is very different from judgment and criticism, which are more reactive.

The ability to sit back, mentally, and take in the whole picture is extremely important. This becomes much easier once we have trained some non-reactivity through mindfulness practice. We can then *consciously* project our attention into the future and past, to plan intentionally and remember accurately. When we do this effectively, expectations become aspirations rather than fixed ideas about what 'must' happen. Just as disciplining ourselves happens most effectively when we simply choose which thoughts to identify with and which to simply ignore, expectations are much more easily met when we focus on the outcome that we want. We can then periodically check in with how we are going as we move toward that aspiration, bringing the honesty and accuracy of perception that comes when we drop judgments and ideas of right/wrong and good/bad and instead see the situation as it is. Often, when people start operating in this way they notice a paradoxical increase in their performance, as they stop getting in their own way with performance anxiety, self-criticism and cynicism toward 'demanding' others.

So making expectations into aspirations is an important first step. We can then be more open to learning from our failures and if we learn from them then it's not a failure but a learning opportunity. When we don't take it personally, failing to meet our own or others' expectations is simply information that we need to work harder or try something different. As we become able to look non-judgmentally at what didn't work and mindfully explore the reasons why, we become more effective. When labels of 'good/bad' and 'right/wrong' are removed we can look more closely at 'failures' and learn from them. We might even come to *welcome* failure and setbacks as necessary steps on the path of growth and learning. Like a tree that becomes stronger as it is blown in different directions by the wind, this is how we develop resilience. If we cease trying to avoid setbacks or pretending they didn't happen, we can truly start learning effectively. It might also be good to remember that as educators and parents, modelling learning from failure can be extremely useful for our kids. If beating oneself up is modelled then that is not so helpful.

In the chapter on mindsets we laid out the evidence showing that 'fixed' mindsets tend to lead to catastrophic stress in the face of failure, and that 'growth' mindsets lead to improved performance following setbacks. We also highlighted how these mindsets are learnt from parents and teachers rather than from books. The way we relate to our own adversity therefore has serious implications for how students relate to theirs.

CHAPTER 18

Mindfulness beyond the classroom

Although this book is about education, the importance of mindfulness for teachers and students goes well beyond the classroom. Ultimately it is about our life's education. This chapter will briefly describe a few elements of mindfulness that go well beyond the home, school or university gate.

Mindfulness and self-care

One of the first things we do in our mindfulness programs is to invite participants to reflect on the things they are *already* doing that encourage (or demand) them to be present. Participants give examples of things such as meditating, yoga, martial arts, physical exercise, listening to or playing music, making art, playing with the family or pets, cooking and eating fine food. In general, these things are inherently rewarding and relaxing. There is something intrinsically enjoyable and relaxing about being present, and so activities that encourage this tend to become hobbies that are enjoyed on a regular basis. Because they are times when we are most mindful they refresh and renew us, clear the mind and help us to re-engage with life in a more constructive way. Discussing this up front sets a very important frame for the exploration of mindfulness that follows. It gets people thinking about mindfulness as a way of being in life, rather than simply a meditation practice they do each day for 10 minutes before re-engaging automatic pilot.

Before adopting self-care as a way of life, we have to cross one of the great barriers to self-care that many people experience. This is the belief that self-care is selfish. It's actually the other way around. If we want to care for others in a sustainable way then we need to learn to care for ourselves. Another barrier is the idea that 'I don't have time for self-care'. Again, it's the other way around. A little time invested in self-care can save a huge amount of time in dealing with the illness, inefficiency and misery that comes with not caring adequately for ourselves. And research increasingly shows that when we care for ourselves and experience positive emotions, our thinking becomes more flexible and we become able to respond to situations in more creative ways.[1] We really have to be very unmindful to ignore the need for self-care.

Looking after ourselves — for example, by getting enough sleep, eating well, drinking enough water, exercising, socialising, finding meaning in what we do and doing more of what is meaningful — is vital to living a happy, healthy life. Sadly, however, the pace and demands of modern life mean that sometimes these things get neglected. If we take a moment to reflect we might notice how being busy can mean we neglect to do things that are nourishing and give life the richness and meaning we want it to have. And, paradoxically, we tend to do this at exactly the times when we need self-care the most.

When we start practising mindfulness we become more aware of our bodies and minds. We may discover tension that a moment before we had no idea was there. When we extend the attentiveness of the formal meditation practice into our daily lives we start to make important discoveries, such as that we hold tension in our body throughout the day, we hold our breath when we are tense or concentrating, or we sit hunched at our desk. Initially this can lead to the awkwardness that comes with being self-conscious until the acceptance catches up with the awareness and self-consciousness gives way to a more easy way of just being conscious of ourselves. We also discover how scattered our attention is, how it jumps from one thing to another like a monkey, is rarely present, tries to do too many things, worries, dwells and creates stress for us through the ways it relates to what is happening. Then we notice the same thing occurring in our lives but, importantly, in realising we are no longer a slave to these habits, we are presented with a choice: continue with these unconscious habits or do something different. Without awareness there is little opportunity for self-care because we are not seeing what is happening.

This translates itself into the rest of our lives. We remember the things that fill us with inspiration and joy, which help us to be most present or help us to relax.

The 'attention training' aspect of mindfulness can, by itself, seem a little cold. Jon Kabat-Zinn, who has been more influential than any other single person in bringing mindfulness into the realm of mainstream healthcare, points out that in Asian languages there are not separate words for 'mind' and 'heart'. Both are referred to with the same word. Thus 'mindfulness' can equally be thought of as 'heartfulness'. The word mindfulness implies 'mind' — which many people equate to the brain — and so risks missing what is most important about learning to be more awake, open and loving in each moment of life.

Caring for the body

Notice what happens when you bring your attention back into your body. You might slow down your walking pace and notice the things around you. Most people who intentionally do this find that their posture changes so that their whole body walks as a single integrated unit rather than being led around by the head. For the same reason, getting out into nature — whether bushwalking or just going for a stroll in the local park or by the beach — helps us get more connected with ourselves and less caught up in our heads. This has a lot to do with being in an environment that is not as inherently overstimulating as a city (and especially a school or university). Generally more of the senses are engaged and enlivened.

We have discussed how mindful movement can help us to become more mindful. Things like dance, sport and being physically active all help us appreciate our bodies more, which in turn motivates us to do more for our bodies. People who quit smoking often have a sense that something is missing for them until they start to exercise and realise through their experience that in ceasing to poison their bodies and damage their lungs they have actually gained more than they have lost.

It is also good to start paying more attention to what and how we eat. So many of us eat for comfort or almost 'inhale' our food on the way out the door. Eating with more awareness puts us more in touch with what and how much the body needs. People who adopt a mindful approach to eating commonly report changing their eating habits — being more aware of when they are hungry (and when they are not), eating more slowly, eating less and enjoying food more. Sometimes they become aware of how much sugar or salt is in their food and cut down on their consumption.

Sleep is another area that is often neglected, reflected in the fact that many people doze off during meditation practice or become aware of how in need of rest they are. The busyness of our day, ingesting too much caffeine and sugar, and generally being on 'default mode' all day long triggers the sympathetic nervous system that prepares us for action but most of us have forgotten how to turn it off, which is not so great when we're trying to sleep. Mindfulness can help here. Studies also show that mindfulness improves the ease of getting to sleep and the quality of sleep, which may be one of the main reasons why it has an antidepressant effect.[2] Better quality of sleep means that we get more refreshment from less time asleep. As a result we are more alert and focused for a day's study and our memory works better.

Caring for the mind

We have already covered how mindfulness helps us take a more compassionate, gentle and accepting stance toward ourselves. We will not go into too much additional detail here. What is worth saying, however, is that as we learn to stop fighting with ourselves during our meditation practice, we stop fighting with ourselves during the rest of the day. Many people report being very surprised when they find that they can actually focus better, simply by learning to recognise when their attention wanders off and gently returning it to their schoolwork or teacher, rather than using self-criticism to try to achieve this. Learning to pay attention in this friendlier way not only reduces stress but improves their performance. Practising criticising ourselves simply draws attention to criticism, and what we practise we will get good at.

Caring for the deeper parts of ourselves

Martin Seligman, who is credited with starting the field now referred to as Positive Psychology, talks about three types of happiness. The first of these, pleasure and gratification, comes from doing things we enjoy, such as eating ice-cream or seeing good movies. The second, embodiment of strengths and virtues, is far more resilient, in the sense that even when the ice-cream has run out and the movie has finished our virtues remain. The third type of happiness comes from having a sense of meaning and purpose. This is more resilient still, because if we are in touch we can find meaning in any moment, depending on the way we choose to see it and what course of action we take. We can even find meaning and learn in the most adverse times or biggest mistakes in our lives.

An example of this can be seen in the life of Viktor Frankl, who spent years interned in Nazi concentration camps, yet had enough space in his mind to find meaning in the horrors he experienced. He later wrote in his book, *Man's Search for Meaning*, that his ability to find meaning and remain connected to his values was what allowed him to survive, whereas others who were unable to do this did not. The extent to which we are able to connect with and live from our values, and to make meaning from our experiences, is the extent to which we will be resilient and ultimately happy on a deeper level than simply gratifying ourselves. If we don't learn to pay attention, including to the things we don't like, we will never learn from them.

What would you like your life to be about? What do you want to be remembered for? When we reflect on our values we can check whether the things we do and say in each moment of our life are in line with these or not. Mindfulness helps by providing the necessary space, objectivity and non-reactivity to start noticing this, and also by helping us sit with what arises as we start living more valued lives. The most important things often require the most effort — they don't come easy. If we value social connectedness and love, for instance, we will seek intimacy with others, and this will undoubtedly at times lead to misunderstandings, feeling let down and even heartache. If we value making a contribution, we will probably feel disappointed when we fall short or are thwarted. But having space in our minds not to just react to these feelings or hold grudges, being in touch with our values and being able to find the meaning in failure will help us to keep going.

Social development

During adolescence there is a lot going on emotionally. Observing an emotional state, such as anxiety, and reacting strongly to it is what is called 'emotional reactivity'. While emotional reactivity occurs on a spectrum, from being relatively stable all the way through to frequent meltdowns, adolescence and young adulthood is a time characterised by strong emotions and often difficulty keeping them under control. Learning to understand and work with our emotions is one of the most important capacities we will ever have and we are learning a lot about this during adolescence. From day to day and even moment to moment there can be storms of emotions that seem to erupt suddenly and intensely. Sometimes these storms pass quickly and at other times hang around. At times we can get stuck in these emotional storms, and this can give rise to more significant difficulties such as anxiety and depression.

Much of this relates to changes in the body and the brain, as well as the social world and how we respond to it. You may recall that the brain's prefrontal cortex is heavily involved in learning and also in regulating emotions. It is also one of the last parts of the brain to finish its development and it develops more slowly in males than females, hence some of the impulsive or immature behaviour for which young males are more often known. The prefrontal cortex undergoes a massive growth spurt between the ages of fifteen and 25, forming new connections particularly with the emotion centre (the limbic system) and it comes fully online as people reach their mid to late twenties. Some of its functions develop before others. The capacity for abstract thinking — that is, imagining and thinking about things that are not actually happening in that moment — is one of the earliest prefrontal capacities to develop, meaning that teenagers can more easily imagine all sorts of things that may or may not happen. This imaginative capacity can be good (we can be creative) and also not so good (we worry). The increased capacity for problem solving, combined with hormones and changes in the social world of a typical teen, means that relationships with family cease to be central in life and relationships with peers become what is most important. It is around this time that many start forming romantic relationships, dating and having sex. Such relationships tend to be happening earlier in life than in previous generations and they tend to bring with them some pretty strong feelings without the capacity to deal with them!

Executive function develops late and is involved, among other things, in managing emotional reactions. It does this in various ways, including changing the way we think about things, changing behaviours, avoiding things, distracting ourselves, and suppressing emotional reactions. It turns out that the best kind of emotion regulation is actually mindfulness — learning to 'sit with' emotional reactions. What does this mean in practice? Let's say that something doesn't go our way at home or school and we feel a sudden rise of intense anger towards the person who we feel is responsible. If we are unmindful we will generally have reacted immediately with some harsh words or gone off somewhere and rehearsed an internal dialogue full of vitriol for the person we are angry with. If, on the other hand, we are a little more mindful, we might notice the anger arise, sensations in the body or changes in our breathing; but before we have acted on the anger we have a little distance from it. This allows us to not fight the wave of anger but instead to surf it. We don't have to criticise ourselves for having anger but we don't have to get dumped by the wave of anger either.

For most people it takes years to learn this but research shows that young people can learn this skill to a sophisticated level if they are given the mindfulness tools to do so.[3] Early on we tend to use less adaptive emotion regulation strategies, such as struggling to keep a lid on emotional reactions rather than let them show (suppression), which leads to feeling emotionally cut off from ourselves, anxiety, depression and, later in life, even things such as increased heart disease.

This can, at times, make it hard to get along with others. Obviously, if we can't handle our emotions and are prone to outbursts, or have to avoid people so that we don't get overwhelmed, it makes it hard to form good social relationships. Add to this the fact that the social world in adolescence is changing fundamentally, and suddenly we have a recipe for some very serious difficulties to emerge. This can even happen in a room full of peers, when we start worrying that we don't have anything to say or that we will be judged or ridiculed if we do say something. It is not uncommon to be in a classroom full of people, or sitting around a table full of peers, and feel completely alone. Social isolation is much more a state of mind than being physically alone.

An easy option is to have virtual relationships online which is fine, but if it's a way of avoiding others and is at the expense of learning how to communicate directly with other people, then living an online persona removed from our real one can compound the problem rather than solve it. The increasing use of technology and social media has replaced actual face-to-face connection and communication for many people exactly at the time when they need direct connection. Trends show that people of all ages are increasingly communicating online: texting rather than speaking, posting invites to events rather than actually inviting people. While this has some significant benefits it can also create a number of pretty serious problems. First of all, people who naturally feel a little anxious socially can find themselves retreating into a world of pseudo-socialising, where they can *think* they are communicating with peers but are actually extremely socially isolated. Communication skills potentially suffer as people start using texts and personal messaging as their primary communication medium. There is something very valuable about being in social situations that bring up strong feelings — even if these feelings are unpleasant — and learning to work with these. Sitting in our bedroom, alone at a computer, with the ability to edit everything we say and alt-tab or write 'BRB' ('be right back' for those of you over the age of twenty) when feelings we don't like come up means that we don't develop the ability to regulate our emotions properly.

In his writings on forming successful intimate relationships, David Schnarch talks at length about what he calls differentiation, which refers to the ability to remain in close contact with others without losing your centre.[4] 'Losing your centre' might include things such as feeling clingy, having to seek approval from others or having a strong need to conform to a group even when the things we are conforming to don't sit well with our real values. Differentiation requires the ability to know who you are without having that reflected back from other people, and also necessitates being able to sit with strong emotions without needing to close off emotionally or bail from the situation. It is, according to Schnarch, a capacity that we continue developing well into middle age, and that some of us never actually get the hang of. Mindfulness makes differentiation, self-esteem and self-reliance easier because we are not so moved by negative and insecure patterns of thought.

As we cultivate awareness of ourselves and others, as well as emotional non-reactivity, openness and kindness, we become better able to relate to others in a similar kind of way. As we become increasingly aware of our own foibles and fears, and relate to them in a more compassionate way, it helps us to empathise better with others who are in the same boat. As we become better able to accept and let go, we become able to tolerate different viewpoints and so can relate to people with more tolerance and less conflict. Communicating with presence has the power to transform communication and relationships. Being present to ourselves and others means that we become more connected with our families, peers, communities and societies.

The phrase 'emotional intelligence' is often shortened to EQ to contrast it with IQ. EQ, as popularised by Daniel Goleman, refers in general to the ability to identify and work with our own emotions as well as those of others. There is a significant and obvious overlap with mindfulness, although they are not the same thing. EQ might be seen as one of the capacities that comes with being truly mindful.

Taking a breath when we are becoming overwhelmed is such an effective intervention, not just for stress reduction but also for improving social development. It gives us that little bit of space necessary to *choose* our response, which is why mindfulness in the classroom is so important not just for learning and resilience but also for whole-person development. We frequently hear participants in our mindfulness courses say that the mindful communication that occurs in each session is one of the most powerful parts of the experience for them. This includes people truly listening to each other rather than rehearsing what to say while waiting for their turn to speak, and people really seeking to communicate their truth with authenticity, rather than hiding parts of themselves to avoid judgment. This means there needs to be an atmosphere of trust and emotional safety as well as shared values of a group or class in order to communicate in this way.

Ethics, values and goals

Some ask, if mindfulness is just about attention then where do ethics and values fit in? If it's just about being in the present moment then where do future goals fit in? These are important questions and we will try to convey why we believe that mindfulness, in the fullest sense of the word, doesn't ignore but rather encompasses and informs ethics, values and goals.

The world's great wisdom traditions say much about the importance of being awake and aware, but they also have much to say about living a life that is underpinned by ethics, morals and values. It would not make much sense if these two important domains of personal or spiritual life were not related. So, how are they related? Well, that might make more sense if we consider what it means to pay attention and be awake — *really* awake!

If mindfulness is just seen as attention or focus in a superficial or narrow sense it could be suggested that a sniper, for example, is very mindful in terms of being able to focus on a target and kill someone. In fact, mindfulness could be argued to make them a more efficient killer than they otherwise would have been. Fair comment. In fact, mindfulness practices are currently being adapted by the military for exactly this purpose.

But what does it mean to really pay attention? If attention is just about the target then mindfulness does seem to be devoid of the values that make such an act cruel or unjust. If, on the other hand, mindfulness is about paying attention in a far more complete and profound way, then being mindful might be the very thing that would prevent the person pulling the trigger. If, for example, such an act was motivated by a fixation on a fanatical ideal at the expense of the bigger picture, then being less attached to and influenced by fanaticism would help prevent the act. As Winston Churchill said: 'A fanatic is one who can't change his mind and won't change the subject.' Furthermore, if such an act was excused by justification of past wrongs or future desires, to the point that the person was not paying attention to what was really taking place in the present moment when they were pulling the trigger, then being truly present may be the opening which allows a little conscience in.

So mindfulness can inhibit us committing a wrong act but can it also positively promote what is known as right action? Absolutely. Acting mindfully is not just a matter of moving away from what is not useful but of positively moving towards what is useful. For example, wisdom traditions from East to West have had much to say about compassion and variously formulated the golden rule of treating others with the same care as we would be treated ourselves. Now, this could just be a pragmatic, secular rule that makes life flow a little easier in society, but it has a deeper meaning than that. When we are most present and aware of the person, animal or planet in front of us then we experience a level of connection that is not normally apparent to us. There is a kind of melting of our usual ego boundaries that keep us imprisoned in our own private world in our heads and separate from the people and world around us. In this sense, mindfulness leads to an experience of oneness which guides our relationships with other humans and animals and governs our treatment of the environment. We get shocked when we see cruelty, as if we can't believe the person perpetrating that cruel act is unable to see what they are doing. Well, in a way they can't, nor can we when we act cruelly. We are, in a manner of speaking, blinded by something. When connected, treating our 'neighbour' as oneself is not an aspiration, it's just a statement of fact because the neighbour is oneself. It's like seeing things in a totally different perspective, as Albert Einstein said:

A human being is a part of the whole, called by us 'Universe,' a part limited in time and space. He experiences himself, his thoughts and feelings as something separated from the rest — a kind of optical delusion of his consciousness. This delusion is a kind of prison for us, restricting us to our personal desires and to affection for a few persons nearest to us. Our task must be to free ourselves from this prison by widening our circle of compassion to embrace all living creatures and the whole of nature in its beauty. Nobody is able to achieve this completely, but the striving for such achievement is in itself a part of the liberation and a foundation for inner security.

We could also consider any ethical principle, value or virtue: justice, honesty, courage, moderation and loyalty to name a few. Although there are many historical and cultural differences in ethics and values, the core principles are more or less similar throughout history and across different cultures. Why might this be so? It may well be that these principles are imprinted in our very being, into our DNA, into the fabric of society. If it weren't, we wouldn't survive for very long as a species let alone as a society. Yes, there is much in our upbringing and culture that can distort it, but it is there. Connecting with that core is a matter of being in touch with ourselves and freeing ourselves from the unconscious and habitual influences that hinder rather than support ethical or valued action. Being cruel to others, for example, doesn't help us to feel at peace within ourselves. There might be some kind of momentary perverse satisfaction if we feel bitter or are incapable of controlling anger, but, like rubbing an eye with a piece of sand in it, what feels good for a moment feels worse very soon after. The remedy is to remove the sand and not to keep rubbing. On the other hand, treating others with care not only helps society to function better but, if we pay attention, we feel better when we do it. This is more of an expression of mindfulness than just being able to focus on our studies in the lead-up to an exam.

According to Socrates, we do not act unethically knowingly or from higher motivation; we do so unknowingly and from a lower motivation such as greed, ignorance, delusion, selfishness or fear. For example, we might think that we gain in business by being greedy or dishonest, but we probably haven't really looked very carefully. We might think we gain by saying something even more cruel in response to someone else's cruelty, but we have just been dragged down to a level of behaviour which we feel unhappy about. We might be self-absorbed about such actions but we cannot call them truly conscious actions because if we were truly conscious and saw the implications of what we were doing we wouldn't do it. When we act unjustly we may or may not harm someone else, but we most certainly harm ourselves. For this reason it is not surprising that the fear and stress centres in the brain are very active when being aggressive or lying (the polygraph, or lie detector test, is actually a test measuring the stress response). It is also not surprising that we feel more relaxed when we act more thoughtfully. Mind you, there is also nothing particularly mindful about self-righteousness.

Being truly self-aware, and being aware of others and our relationship to them, quite naturally leads to ethics and values. It provides us with the opportunity to use our conscience (con: 'to connect with'; and science: 'knowledge'), which means to connect with that quiet inner or intuitive knowledge in all of us that simply knows what is right or wrong in any given situation. Often we do not hear that intuitive knowledge because we are too distracted and mentally busy. It is only noticed when we are inwardly quiet, and in such situations having a 'good authority' to refer to might help.

We do not have to go about our day-to-day life for too long to realise that we don't always act in ways we are proud of. Although mindfulness teaches us not to criticise ourselves, it can help us to notice the motivation for our actions, and the effect those actions had on us afterwards. We can learn from this and therefore make increasingly informed choices in the future.

The other issue of how mindfulness relates to goals is worth considering. Although mindfulness is very much about the present it also encompasses goals. When we hold a goal in mind then that goal is here, now. We may make a present-moment decision to head towards that goal, to dedicate time to it or to involve others in it. The important thing is to note:

- that the goal is consistent with our deeper values
- it is feasible and worthwhile
- it doesn't override other, more important goals
- that we consciously navigate towards it, responsive to moment-by-moment circumstances
- we don't get so preoccupied with the destination that we forget to enjoy the journey.

Mindful parents, mindful kids

As children, we all had experiences where we were talking to our teachers or parents but could tell that their minds were elsewhere, perhaps still at the office or maybe mentally compiling a shopping list, or maybe as they multitasked while absentmindedly reassuring us that they were listening. We could tell they were not listening by the blank, faraway look in their eyes, or perhaps because of their pat, shallow responses to our fascination about something. Even though we may have sworn to ourselves that we would never be like that, fast forward a couple of decades and we might find ourselves doing exactly that!

Unfortunately, when as a parent or teacher we don't pay attention to a child, then through modelling we are unconsciously teaching unmindfulness to them. There is no point in telling a child to pay attention if we are not paying attention ourselves. Many young people come to communicate and interact in this way. Perhaps some of that can be attributed to the busyness of modern life and the effects of technology and social media, but it is certain that some of it is a result of parents and teachers interacting with *them* in ways that lack true connection and presence. In this way, unmindfulness becomes a generational problem.

Notice what happens next time you are walking around happy, with a big smile, and compare this to the experience of walking around with a storm cloud over your head and a big scowl. You probably already know the difference between these two experiences, but if not, check it out. We get instant feedback: smile, and the whole world smiles with you, as the song goes. The same thing holds when parents relate to kids but it is amplified, since children look up to adults and particularly their parents for guidance and direction. A misguided and directionless (unmindful) parent means contributing towards a misguided and directionless child.

Right from the beginning, how we interact with children changes their brain and alters the course of their development. Research shows that babies as young as four months old can recognise emotions in their mother's face.[5] Children whose mother's (or other primary caregiver's) interactions with them are intimate and nurturing are far more resilient and happy in later life, which speaks to the utmost importance of mindful communication with children.[6] Studies have even shown that significant stress for a woman during pregnancy can have an effect on how the developing child's DNA expresses itself, making the future child more likely to have issues with anxiety and depression as well as making the DNA of the child age faster.[7,8] So care for the child means care for the parents, especially the mother, right from and even before conception.

The main message is, in order to teach a child mindfulness we should practise it ourselves. We can make our children themselves the object of our mindfulness practice when we fully attend to a child in each moment — paying close attention to what they are saying, how they are saying it, how they hold themselves and their facial expression. Many parents in our mindfulness courses have told us that when they do this, their children enjoy the contact and mutual communion for a few minutes and then go back to what they were doing before. Spending a few moments *really* connected to our children is worth infinitely more than any amount of time being physically present yet with our minds a million miles away.

Multitasking while speaking to children is one of the greatest barriers to really connecting: for example, trying to make the lunches while barking orders to get ready to a six-year-old while they are trying to show you something about which they are fascinated. We might say, 'Yes, I am looking!' but we won't fool the child. That moment's attention may well save hours of attention-seeking behaviour because children often have to make a lot of noise to get a parent's attention. Being mindful with a child, especially an adolescent, can also mean not going into a conversation with a set agenda and fixed ideas about how things should go. It can totally upset spontaneous, authentic and open communication.

A mother gave the example of being up late one night breastfeeding her child. She said she felt tired and resentful of having to be up late and was already anticipating being tired the next day. Then she remembered mindfulness and stopped giving her attention to the endless trains of thought and gave it fully to the baby quietly feeding. Unexpectedly, resentment gave way to love and tiredness gave way to peace and restfulness. She needed to remain mindful however, because the next train of thought to come in was of guilt about being a resentful mother; that train goes nowhere useful. A father gave another example of how mindfulness had helped him to be much more patient with himself, and this flowed onto being much more attentive in listening to his teenage children. A side effect was that he was much less irritable with them at the end of his day's work.

An important role of parenthood is to cultivate an environment that makes it easy for children to be mindful. Just as a parent chooses the food for a child when they shop at the market, a parent has a responsibility to choose the food for the child's mind in terms of what sort of literature, music or media will be chosen in the home environment. For example, very noisy and fast-paced stimuli (e.g. cartoons or music) will have a negative effect on attention and the development of executive function in children exposed to them.[9]

Just as students spending time each day meditating is an investment in their own productivity, time spent connecting with our children can be viewed as an opportunity to train our capacity for awareness, which in turn improves our performance at work, which obviously means that we can then *really* afford to let go of thoughts of the office when we get home at night, creating the kind of feedback loop that makes mindfulness such a self-sustaining and valuable way of being in the world.

Creating a mindful society

It is perhaps very fitting that the original centre for mindfulness that was formed by Jon Kabat-Zinn is named the University of Massachusetts Medical School Center for Mindfulness in Medicine, Health Care, and Society.[10] Most people get the medicine and healthcare parts, but the aim is for mindfulness to provide benefit to people right across all areas of society.

Earlier in this book we explored the individual costs of unmindfulness, which were significant and included: wasting time; not understanding things; mental roadblocks; poor emotional wellbeing; not enjoying life; inability to sleep well; communicating poorly; being more easily distracted; lack of motivation; poor memory; and negative effects on the brain. A society is only a collection of individuals and is made up of the same human nature, so those individual costs could as easily be listed as the collective costs of an unmindful society, such as:

- Potentially we waste huge amounts of time and resources with indiscriminate and ineffective action and poor decision-making.
- Governments and electorates that become distracted and reactive are far more easily misled and often make poor decisions.

We experience confusion on a major scale and then find it difficult to work collectively together towards a goal even when there is a pressing need.

The global financial crisis, or GFC, is a classic example of economies and societies having found themselves in a perilous situation, originally through not paying attention to or reading the signposts that were obvious in the past. Now those same societies that are the most vulnerable to debt are tearing themselves apart, almost paralysed with conflict and inertia despite being in pain. Collective and cooperative action is almost impossible.

Our collective emotional wellbeing has been declining for around 60 years with depression in particular predicted to be the developed world's number one burden of disease by the year 2030, despite the fact that over that time we have been living in a period of unprecedented economic affluence.[11] Added to this are other mental health problems such as anxiety and an increasingly addiction-prone society.

There are a lot of reasons behind poor mental health but isolation, a lack of meaning, a less balanced lifestyle and poor sleep are some important reasons.

The volume of communication in the world today has been greatly enhanced by the use of modern technologies but there are growing levels of isolation and probably less understanding than previously.

There has been a collective rise in distractibility and attention deficit problems with the resort to, and overuse of, medications to treat it. The causes of the problems so far have remained relatively unaddressed.

Although society inevitably changes and evolves, a society that has lost touch with its traditions, institutions and history both loses its soul and is destined to repeat past mistakes.

The aim is not so much to paint an overly gloomy picture of the world but rather to acknowledge the problems that we collectively face and, just as for the individual, to develop the circumstances in which we can solve them. The ingredients include objectively seeing what those problems are, cultivating the insight to identify the solutions to those problems, and having the courage and determination to collectively carry those solutions into action. In order to create a more mindful society we need to first recognise what it costs us if we don't. Although it will take some time and energy to do it, the alternative to not cultivating mindfulness will be far greater in the long run. Although the following quote is of uncertain origin, and although it applies to the whole human race and not just Americans, it is rather apt in relation to the integration of mindfulness. 'Americans [human beings] can always be counted on to do the right thing … after they have exhausted all other possibilities.'

Cultivating a more mindful society could be done in a number of ways, involving different groups and levels of society each with their own particular needs. Important ingredients include the following.

Research

The explosion of interest in mindfulness has been on the back of increasingly high quality research and evidence. Such research is important for a range of reasons, including helping people to understand the importance of mindfulness and to guide and inform its effective and responsible application. Such research needs to be funded and prioritised by the funding bodies that make decisions on where research money goes. This requires more informed and enlightened policymakers.

Education and training

Education needs to take place at a number of levels, starting with the training of quality mindfulness teachers within schools, universities, education faculties and organisations. If the teachers of mindfulness are well taught then the people they train are likely to be well taught also. The suite of programs on offer at Monash University, delivered by the authors and a growing body of passionate, skilled facilitators, gives an example of how mindfulness can be integrated into an organisation.[12] There is no one correct model for this and each organisation needs to evolve its own programs sensitively according to need and context.

Healthcare

Because of its range of health-based applications, one of the main demand areas for mindfulness-based interventions will always be in healthcare. It can be used as a primary therapy in itself or as an adjunct to other therapies, whether it be in primary to tertiary healthcare settings by medical and allied health practitioners including doctors, psychologists, psychiatrists, physiotherapists, occupational therapists, nurses and dieticians. The range of conditions for which it has application includes mental health problems (e.g. depression, anxiety, panic disorder, sleep problems, eating disorders and psychosis), pain management, chronic illness (e.g. cancer, heart disease and autoimmune conditions), as well as for its physical effects (e.g. metabolic, immunity, genetic and neurological).

Business

An increasing number of businesses and financial organisations are becoming interested in mindfulness for a range of reasons such as improvements in staff wellbeing, productivity, leadership, teamwork, decision making, communication, service delivery, and adapting to organisational change. Although delivering such programs could be seen as a business expense, it is more useful to see it as an investment that will deliver far more in the long run than it costs.

Leadership

Because of the qualities associated with mindfulness (such as greater emotional intelligence, performance, executive functioning and resilience, as well as reducing career fatigue and burnout) there is a lot of interest in what mindfulness training has to offer in the training of effective leaders. In a world where leadership often looks to be anything but mindful there is a pressing need for more of this work in setting the tone of a community or workplace.

Communication and outreach

With the increase of mindfulness-based literature and research it is important that this information be available and communicated in relevant and effective ways. This includes online and app-based delivery, as well as via more traditional forms of communication such as through books and CDs. Online and app-based mindfulness programs have the advantage of reaching a wide audience for relatively little cost but have the disadvantage of not having the face-to-face contact of a student and teacher, where questions and concerns can be voiced, encouragement given and qualities of mindfulness embodied rather than explained. There needs to be a wide variety of methods to suit the range of age groups and individual preferences.

Politics and public policy

For mindfulness to be disseminated effectively to those who need it, we need to create a conducive climate as well as find the resources to do it. This is the role of governments, education departments, the legal profession and business leaders. This will also need to include professional bodies who can oversee standards, ethics, training and regulations governing mindfulness teachers. Such bodies already exist for the teaching of meditation.[13,14]

CHAPTER 19

Organisational approaches to mindfulness

By now we hope that you can see why mindfulness in education is a good idea. What school or university wouldn't want to simultaneously improve wellbeing and performance? And when the possibility of whole-person development and spiritual growth for the students (and staff, also) is thrown into the mix, it becomes a 'no-brainer'. This is why a number of educational institutions have now started introducing mindfulness to the curriculum. This ranges from 5-minute mindfulness meditation sessions in the morning or after lunch all the way up to structured 6-week courses. Some have even gone further and are finding ways to roll out mindfulness across the entire organisation, creating mindful learning environments.

Both the authors are centrally involved in doing this at Monash University in Melbourne, Australia, and regularly consult to other schools and universities who are busy doing the same. This is a move towards creating the mindful school, mindful university and, hopefully, the mindful society. In this chapter, we describe how this is being achieved at Monash. We then outline practical considerations that can help organisations embed mindfulness in their curriculum and organisational culture in a way that is effective and sustainable.

The Monash story

One of the authors (Craig Hassed) began teaching in the Monash medical faculty in 1989. Soon he was running optional lunchtime mindfulness meditation sessions, and then elective courses with the intention of expanding this into the medical curriculum. This required finding a rationale for introducing it into the core curriculum for trainee doctors, as well as finding a language that retained the integrity of mindfulness yet also made it accessible to a critical, scientific audience. Coincidentally, in 1991, stress became identified as a significant problem amongst medical students and resources were channelled into addressing this. The mindfulness–based Stress Release Program (SRP) had been developed for doctors and was adapted to teaching medical students with a focus on their needs and issues, but also to help them understand how this could be used with patients. In 2002, the SRP was expanded into the Health Enhancement Program (HEP), which incorporated both a core mindfulness-based stress reduction component and more formal education around lifestyle factors such as exercise, sleep, nutrition and connectedness.

The HEP was well received and expanded so that core principles were revisited in the second and third year of the medical course. The SRP was picked up by Harvard University as an elective for their medical students as well as being delivered by other educational institutions, both domestic and international, as they became interested in the model being pioneered at Monash.[1]

Popular courses for Monash staff and students outside of the medical faculty (such as Mindfulness for Academic Success) were also offered at Monash but then, in 2010, after a series of successful meetings with key figures within the university, a decision was made to expand and fund the mindfulness initiative out of medicine and into the wider university. Mindfulness was formally established within the Monash Mental Health Review strategy, and support grew further. Both authors are now employed as consultants by Monash and are actively involved in educating the university community about the benefits of mindfulness, developing and providing programs, conducting research and training mindfulness facilitators within the university and in other institutions. The grand vision is to embed mindfulness in the core curriculum to improve the mental health, resilience and performance of all Monash students and staff. William James would have been proud!

Making it organic

The approach at Monash has been graded and 'organic' in that it grew as the environment supported and demanded it. We have emphasised promoting mindfulness in an evidence-based, practical way, and then providing workshops and programs to interested parties, rather than attempting to force it on people who are not ready.

There are a number of problems with trying to do too much, too soon. Some educational institutions we consult to have attempted to roll out mindfulness unilaterally, for instance requiring teachers who might not be ready to run meditation sessions to do so and expecting students to engage with it. This has been enabled by the wide array of resources currently available, such as Smiling Mind, a mindfulness app and website, the development of which the authors were involved in.[2] Many schools are using this as a resource, since it allows plug-and-play mindfulness meditation sessions, taking the burden off teachers to facilitate the actual meditation sessions. However, as can be expected, some teachers and students engage with mindfulness more willingly than others. This is especially the case when mindfulness is presented as something that students and teachers 'have' to do, rather than presented in a way that makes it obvious why they would want to start using it. If teachers are not engaged and motivated then that is what will be communicated to students.

We recommend that organisations roll out mindfulness in a considered, 'organic' way. It is important to communicate clearly to students, staff and parents what mindfulness is and how it can be helpful. This is best done with evidence to support it, by making it relevant and using plain language. This increases buy-in and decreases resistance. Practical tips are given below for communicating clearly what mindfulness is and how it can help students academically and personally.

Once everyone understands exactly what mindfulness is (and isn't) and also how it can be brought into the classroom both formally (through meditation sessions) and informally (through encouraging mindful communication and learning styles), students generally tend to start learning more effectively. Grades improve, problem behaviours reduce, and the use of mindfulness in the classroom becomes an obvious benefit. Ultimately, the evidence that comes from experience is far more important than anything we can read in a book.

Spending 5 minutes meditating in the morning or after lunch then becomes an investment in student welfare and academic performance (not to mention teacher wellbeing!), and it becomes self-sustaining. Other students and staff then tend to become interested, and it starts to snowball. Formal evaluation of the effects of mindfulness on student welfare and performance also facilitates this.

Communicating the message

It is extremely important that the first experience people have of mindfulness is a positive one. The authors of this book both adhere to the maxim that it is better to provide no experience of mindfulness than to provide a bad one. It is all too easy for people to think that mindfulness is a waste of time — pointless navel gazing — or a way to avoid thoughts or feelings. As a general consideration, the first experience of mindfulness that any student has ought to be short (i.e. 5 minutes or so), clearly explained, and made instantly relevant to their studies. Take time to debrief and learn from what works and what doesn't.

We suggest that students, teachers and parents are, if possible, all provided with a clear rationale for using mindfulness in the classroom. It can be useful to start by discussing the nature of default mode, which occurs when we are not paying attention. It can also be useful to outline the costs of default-mode unmindfulness (i.e. inattention and distraction), including increased incidence of physical and mental health problems, impaired relationships and decreased performance. We then tend to introduce mindfulness as the remedy for this.

We refer to 'everyday' or 'accidental' experiences of mindfulness, such as spontaneous moments of presence while watching sunsets, eating new foods and so on, and go on to distinguish these from mindfulness meditation. It is generally a good idea to then give people an experience of mindfulness meditation. If facilitated skilfully, guiding them through a 5-minute body scan can give them a very direct, felt sense of the way that simply paying attention to one's body can produce relaxation, a sharpening of attentional focus and increased insight (e.g. of just how much the mind wanders when we try to pay attention). It can be good to get people to reflect on what is different for them having done the practice (we ask them to 'notice what is different for you now, having paid attention to your body in this way for 5 minutes'), and it can even be quite useful to get a show of hands of people in the audience who experienced each of these things.

As was covered in Chapter 2, there is a large and rapidly increasing evidence base around the benefits of mindfulness for things like reducing stress, increasing resilience and improving cognitive (and, therefore, academic) performance. It is helpful to reference this in any presentation on mindfulness, especially to more critical audiences such as older students, other teachers or parents. It can also be helpful to discuss the evidence around the costs of unmindfulness.

Mindfulness fatigue

We have noticed through our work with both Monash and other organisations that when mindfulness is presented to students in a way that is not clear, practical and relevant, they sometimes go on to develop a resistance to it later. For instance, some schools that require all students to meditate in the mornings find that after some time, the students have an attitude of 'yes, we get mindfulness ... we need to pay attention', but that this doesn't translate to actual increases in presence or performance. We term this phenomenon 'mindfulness fatigue' and believe that it results primarily from a superficial, intellectual understanding of mindfulness. The giveaway is that it tends to occur alongside an attitude of 'We have "done" mindfulness now, so what's next?'. This attitude is obviously antithetical to the whole character of mindfulness, and is a sure sign that the students (and, often, teachers) have not grasped mindfulness on a deeper level.

Mindfulness can then be introduced into the classroom. Considerations when doing this are that it should be done slowly, with short meditations (e.g. 1 or 2 minutes for young children and 5 minutes for older ones). If a student doesn't want to practise the meditation while the group is, they can be encouraged to just rest for a while. Even 5 minutes of meditation first thing in the morning (e.g. during home room) or immediately after lunch will help settle and focus students and make them more effective learners. This will most likely produce noticeable improvements in performance within a short time. It can be useful to ask students about what improvements they have begun noticing as this amplifies the experience for them, and bringing it out in a group discussion can motivate other students who have not yet opened to mindfulness. In time, these improvements are also likely to be noticed by students in other classes, as well as staff, who will hopefully then become interested in personally applying mindfulness.

In general, it is useful to start small, getting key stakeholders on board by giving them positive experiences of mindfulness and an invitation to use it personally to enhance their own wellbeing. The next step is to support their use of it in the classroom, providing resources (such as audio recordings of mindfulness meditations and written resources) and allocating time. The benefits of mindfulness can then slowly but surely go viral, until ultimately the whole organisation directly experiences the benefits of mindfulness.

For staff, meetings can begin and end with a brief time of mindfulness practice to help focus and settle. Concepts such as letting go, acceptance and the present moment will become part of the organisational language and culture. Teachers, once they have a deeper understanding of mindfulness, can also become creative in introducing it into things like sports practice, science or biology classes, and art lessons.

Soon mindfulness will find its way into the fabric of the place as it finds a place in the heart of the individuals who work and study there.

CHAPTER 20

The exercises

The following exercises are designed to help bring the ideas in this book to life. As we have emphasised throughout, mindfulness is experiential and there is no substitute for actually doing the practice and noticing the effects of each exercise on your wellbeing and performance.

These exercises may also be used as resources for teachers interested in bringing mindfulness into their classroom. It will be best to practise them yourself a few times so as to gain familiarity with them before attempting to guide a group through them.

Experiment with them and find your own style for reading them out. Remember that there is no right or wrong way to guide mindfulness practices, although keeping them simple and clear is generally best. Remember that mindfulness is about becoming more aware and awake, and so a tone of voice that is clear and invites presence and impartiality is better than a soft, hypnotic voice that invites sleepiness. For the same reason, we suggest sitting up and practising in well-lit rooms (or outside) rather than dimming the lights. Also practise being mindful yourself as you are teaching it.

In the scripts below, spaces and '…' between the text indicate that you should take your time with the exercise, either when doing it yourself or reading it aloud to students. They indicate that you should bring a sense of considered calm to your practice. Obviously '(pause)' denotes a suitable time to allow a longer space. When people are beginning to practise mindfulness, it can be good to provide a little more guidance and gentle prompts to bring their attention back. As they become familiar with mindfulness, you can start leaving longer pauses and providing less guidance.

After you familiarise yourself with these practices, you might like to start improvising your own. DIY mindfulness is actually easy and straightforward once you have grasped the basics. Essentially, you can choose anything that is happening in the five senses and invite people to gently rest their attention with that object. Encourage them to notice when their attention wanders and to bring it back, giving themselves permission for this mind wandering to occur. Emphasise generating a sense of acceptance and openness to whatever arises while practising.

Exercise 1: Body scan

This is a practice called the body scan, which you can make as long or short as you have time for. Put more or less space between the instructions depending on how long you intend to practise for. As you take others through the practice, practise being mindful yourself.

Script

You can do this exercise sitting on a chair or cross-legged on a cushion on the floor. You can also lie down — but make an effort that you don't go to sleep. Mindfulness is about becoming more aware and more awake, not zoning out or getting sleepy. Make sure your back is straight but without tension. This will keep you more alert. If you are sitting on a chair, it's best to have both feet resting comfortably on the floor.

Now close your eyes, or half close them if that is more comfortable for you, without looking at anything in particular. Take a moment to settle into this posture ...

Begin by feeling your whole body, sitting where it is ...

Noticing the boundaries of your body ... your skin, where it touches your clothes or the air around you ... perhaps noticing the differences between them in terms of temperature and texture ...

And becoming aware of your posture, the way that you are sitting ... noticing how you can sense which parts of your body are bent and which parts are straight, without needing to look at them ...

And now feeling the contact that your legs and back make with the chair ... letting the chair support your weight ... and noticing how as you let the chair support you, there are muscles turned on in your body that don't need to be ... for instance in your face ... your hands ... your feet ... letting go of any tension that you notice in those areas ... and letting your body settle into this simple sitting posture ...

Now feeling your feet on the floor ... tuning in to the sense of groundedness and stability that comes from having your feet squarely on the floor ... this is something you can tune into anytime, anywhere ... your feet are often touching the ground and this is a way to bring your attention into the present ...

Perhaps noticing how, as you feel your body in this way, your attention has already started to settle more in the present moment ...

Now bringing your attention to the soles of your feet ... literally feeling them touching the ground ... maybe through your shoes and socks ... and just noticing the sensations that are showing up there right now ...

Perhaps you feel a lot of different sensations ... or maybe a few really intense sensations ... or maybe you are aware of an absence of sensations, of numbness ... there is no right or wrong here ... whatever you are feeling right now on the soles of your feet, just noticing that ... see if you can let those sensations just be there, exactly as they are, without trying to change them or do anything about them ...

And now expanding your awareness to also feel the rest of your feet ... your toes ... your instep ... heels ... ankles ... so now just holding both feet in awareness ...

And also both legs ... your shins ... calves ... knees ... thighs ... hamstrings ... buttocks ... So now holding both legs and both feet in awareness ... just feeling what is there to be felt ...

From time to time your mind will wander off ... into daydreaming, thinking about what you are going to do later, or thinking about what you were doing before ... or making up stories about what is happening now ... that is totally normal, it happens to everyone ... any time that you notice your mind has wandered off, just observe where it has gone to and gently return your attention to your legs and feet ...

And if it wanders off a hundred times, just bring it back a hundred times ... practise being patient with yourself as you practise paying attention ... Now letting go of your legs and feet ... and moving your attention to your hands ... noticing what you can feel on the palms of your hands ... and the backs of your hands ... maybe the difference in temperature between them ... just be aware of whatever is there to be noticed ... feeling your thumbs ... and fingers ... and holding both hands in awareness now ...

And also both arms ...

Simply present to whatever is showing up on these parts of your body right now ... seeing if you can greet all sensations in the same way — whether they are weak or intense, pleasant or unpleasant — with acceptance that that is what is showing up right now ... with a sense of openness and friendliness ...

Simply noticing any time your mind wanders off, and gently bringing your attention back to your arms and hands ... practising being kind to yourself as you do so ...

Now shifting your attention to your stomach ... without changing your breath in any way, just noticing the natural expansion and contraction of your stomach as your body breathes in and out all by itself ...

And also feeling your chest ...

And your back ... and so holding your trunk in awareness ... aware of all the sensations showing up right now ... feeling the surface of your body, where your skin touches your clothes ... and then taking your awareness in deeper ... in through the layers of muscle and bones and right into your organs ... into the core of your body ... bathing your whole trunk in awareness ...

Then moving your attention to your shoulders ... and neck ...

This is an area where lots of us hold tension, so if you become aware of any tensing or bracing, just letting go of that ... and then noticing whatever remains ... and greeting that with acceptance and friendliness ... being open to whatever is there ... noticing if your mind labels or judges any of the sensations, or reacts to them ... and just letting go of these reactions and judgments ... so you can feel what is actually there ... tuning in to the actual sensations, rather than what your mind is telling you about them ...

Then noticing your face ... releasing tension in the jaw ... eyes ... eyebrows ... forehead ... and feeling the whole face ... noticing everything that is showing up there right now ...

And then once again noticing your whole body ... sitting ... breathing ... Letting go of any tension that has crept back in ...

And noticing — really noticing — what it feels like to just sit ... and breathe ... and be present ...

Letting thoughts and feelings come and go ... simply holding them all in awareness ... 'awarenessing' whatever happens in each moment ...

(Pause)

And as we start to bring this practice to a close, just noticing what is different for you now ... perhaps you feel more relaxed ... or centred ... or alert ... or perhaps you are aware of agitation or tension that you hadn't noticed before ... whatever is true for you, just acknowledging that ...

And when you are ready, opening your eyes and bringing your attention back more fully to where you are ... and as best you can, holding this increased awareness ... and acceptance ... this mindfulness ... as you go on with whatever you are doing next.

Exercise 2: Using the breath as an anchor

Script

In this simple practice, we will start by focusing on the body to ground us in the present moment. Then we will bring awareness to the breath coming and going in the body from moment to moment. This will give you another tool to help keep your attention in the present, and a reference point to come back to any time your attention wanders off, helping you stay more present and aware throughout the day.

Start by noticing your whole body ...

First of all, just feeling your body ... becoming aware of the state it is in right now... observing whether it is tired ... or alert ... or relaxed ... heavy or light ... whether you can feel it clearly or whether it is hard to feel it ... just noticing how it *is* right now ...

Letting go of any tension that you find anywhere ...

And just letting your body settle into whatever position it is in ... sitting or lying ...

And also becoming aware of your mind ... what thoughts are around ... is your mind calm and present ... or agitated and scattered?

And what feelings do you notice?

Whatever you notice, in your body and your mind, just letting it be there exactly as it is ... not fighting with it ... not trying to change it ... not thinking about it ... just letting it be there ... bringing an attitude of acceptance and friendliness to it ...

And then noticing how it feels to breathe ... feeling the expansion and contraction of your belly ... the rise and fall of your shoulders ... maybe you can even feel the air brushing in and out of your nostrils ...

Taking a few deeper breaths ...

And then just letting your breathing settle into its own rhythm ... letting your body breathe naturally, as it knows how to do and as it does even when you are not paying any attention to it ...

Just noticing how it feels to breathe in ... and out ...

Letting your attention settle on wherever in your body you feel the breath most strongly ... perhaps at the nostrils ... or the chest ... or the belly ...

And simply resting your attention there ... aware of each in-breath and each out-breath ...

(Pause)

Breathing in awareness ... and letting go of any tension on the out-breath ...

Resting your attention lightly on the breath ... not blocking anything out ... or getting too fixed on the breath ... just using it as an anchor to keep your attention in the present ...

Following each breath all the way through — start, middle and end ...

Noticing the point where it turns around ...

Being really *curious* how it feels to breathe …

And any time your attention wanders off — no matter where it goes — simply noticing where it has gone, then gently escorting it back to the breath …

Simply bringing it back over and over and over again, as many times as you need to …

Back to *this* breath … *this* moment … moment by moment … breath by breath …

(Pause)

Just being aware when you're breathing in … and when you're breathing out … Letting go of any tension in your belly … so that your body can just breathe naturally … without any resistance …

Each breath is completely unique … you have never taken *this* breath before, and you never will again … *this* breath … *now* …

(Pause)

Don't worry if it feels like you are controlling your breath a little — this is natural … just noticing this thought — it's just a thought — and continuing to feel what it's like as you breathe in … and out … in … and out …

Just coming back to the breath any time your attention wanders off …

When thoughts arise in the mind, simply noticing them … taking note of what has drawn your attention away from the breath … and gently returning your attention once again to the breath … holding your breathing and whatever distracts you in a spacious awareness …

including everything in the practice ... not trying to change or get rid of anything ...

(Longer pause)

And now expanding your awareness around wherever you were observing the breath ... to include a sense of the body as a whole ... noticing how your whole body is involved in breathing ...

Feeling what it's like to just sit ... and breathe ...

Coming back over and over again ...

This moment ... *this* breath ...

And staying connected to your breath ... gently allowing your eyes to open ...

Noticing what it's like to bring your attention back to your surroundings, while at the same time staying connected with your breath ...

Remembering that this is something you can do at any stage throughout the day, wherever you are, whatever you are doing ... the breath is always there, just like the body ... and it is always a way back into the present moment.

Exercise 3: Tuning in to your surroundings

This practice goes for 15 minutes and helps you to start using all of your senses to ground yourself in the present moment. In particular, we will be focusing on the senses of touch, hearing and vision. You can do it anywhere and any time, indoors or outdoors — you might like to experiment with practising it in different places and noticing the difference.

Script

Start by feeling your whole body. Simply feeling your body, becoming aware of the state that it is in right now. Observe whether it is tired or alert, relaxed or tense, heavy or light. Notice whether you can feel it clearly or whether it is hard to feel. Just noticing how it *is* right now ...

Letting go of any tension that you find anywhere ...

And just letting your body settle into whatever position it is in — sitting or lying ...

And also becoming aware of your mind. What thoughts are around ... is your mind calm and present ... or dull and sleepy ... or agitated and scattered?

Also noticing your feelings and emotions ...

Just acknowledging whatever is there to be acknowledged. Whatever you notice, in your body and your mind, just letting it be there exactly as it is ... without fighting with it or trying to change it ... not thinking about it or trying to figure anything out. Just letting it be there, bringing an attitude of acceptance and friendliness to it ...

And then noticing how it feels to breathe ... feeling the expansion and contraction of your belly, the rise and fall of your shoulders ... maybe you can even feel the air brushing in and out of your nostrils ...

Taking a few deeper breaths ...

And then just letting your breathing settle into its own rhythm ... letting your body breathe naturally, as it knows how to do and as it does even when you are not paying any attention to it ...

Just noticing how it feels to breathe in ... and out ...

Letting your attention rest on wherever in the body your breathing is most obvious ...

(Pause)

Breathing in awareness, letting go of tension on the out-breath ...

Resting your attention lightly on the breath ... not blocking anything out, or getting too fixed on the breath ... just using it as an anchor to keep your attention in the present ...

Following each breath all the way through — start, middle and end ... noticing the point where it turns around ... being really *curious* how it feels to breathe ...

And any time your attention wanders off — no matter where it goes — simply noticing where it has gone, then gently escorting it back to the breath ... and just as with the body scan, bringing it back over and over and over again, as many times as you need to ...

Seeing how quickly you can catch your attention when it sneaks off ...

(Pause)

Just aware when you're breathing in, and when you're breathing out ...

Letting go of any tension in your belly, so that your body can just breathe naturally, without any resistance ...

(Pause)

Noticing any sense that you are controlling your breath a little, or thoughts that you are not breathing properly, or deeply enough … simply seeing these thoughts for what they are — just thoughts — and continuing to notice what it feels like as you breathe in … and out … in … and out …

Simply coming back to the breath any time your attention wanders off … letting thoughts and feelings just come and go from moment to moment, acknowledging their presence but not needing to engage with them in any way …

(Longer pause)

And now letting go of the sense of touch, and bringing your attention to hearing … of course, you will still notice your breath coming and going, and still feel sensations in your body … but now, it is like the spotlight of your attention is on hearing, and everything else — all the sensations, what you can see and smell and taste, and any thoughts and feelings — they can all just be there off in the shadows, while the spotlight of your attention is on hearing …

Just noting all the different sounds around you right now … sounds from close by, maybe even within your own body … and sounds from the room or the space you find yourself in, and from right off into the distance … see if you can become aware of the closest sound as well as the most distant one, holding both in awareness at the same time …

Of course, it's all just vibrations, moving through the air … no sound any more important than the others …

Just sitting in awareness, noticing fully each sound as it comes to you ... aware of the rich soundscape in which you currently find yourself ...

(Pause)

Not searching for any particular sound ... just being actively aware of the soundscape around you ...

Perhaps noticing that your attention has a habit of fixating on particular sounds ... simply noting this has occurred and then coming back to listening to *all* sounds ...

Just listening ...

(Pause)

Noticing the sounds themselves, the points of sound, and the *silence* between the sounds ... experiencing the silence that sounds appear out of and disappear back into ... so you are aware of sounds and silence *at the same time* ...

(Longer pause)

And now gently opening your eyes ... letting go of the sense of hearing, and bringing your attention to what you can *see* ...

Just letting your gaze wander, taking in shapes, and colours ... noticing the way light reflects from certain objects and how other objects cast shadows ...

Noticing movement ... and stillness ...

Not fixating on any particular object, just letting your gaze wander and taking it all in ...

Noticing how your mind tends to label everything you see, to name it and maybe even judge it or think about it ... and as best you can, letting go of any thoughts or labels or judgments ... and *just seeing* ... literally just seeing what is there to be seen.

As you look in this way, with fresh eyes, perhaps noticing how you start to become aware of things that you didn't see before ... this often happens when we bring mindful awareness to what is going on ... when we wake up to each moment, we become aware of new things that we would normally have ignored or failed to notice ...

(Pause)

Any time you notice your attention has wandered off anywhere else, just bringing it back ...

(Pause)

And now just sitting, feeling your body, and your breath coming and going ... and noticing sounds around you, and what you can see, and tuning in to any smells or tastes ... really noticing what it is like to sit ... to simply sit, and be present, from moment to moment, breath to breath ...

Coming back over and over again, to *this* moment ... and *this* one ...

Being the awareness, the mirror that reflects everything but is unchanged by it, the depths of the ocean on which waves come and go ...

(Pause)

Realising how we only ever really *have* moments to live ...

And as we bring the exercise to an end, keeping as much of this awareness as possible as you move off into whatever is next.

Remembering that you can come back to your body, your breathing, to any of your senses, at any time during the day ... any time you find yourself zoning out or getting caught up in negative thinking.

Exercise 4: Expanding your awareness

This practice will take about 15 minutes or so. It uses the senses of touch, hearing and seeing. It is designed to help you be more present in each moment, and to become aware of new things that you would normally not notice.

The more you practise this exercise, the more you will start to notice new details that you were not aware of before. This will help you become even more connected with the present moment, with what is happening around you and within you in each moment, rather than getting caught up in thoughts and reactions.

Script

Start by sitting comfortably, using your body and breath as an anchor to quickly bring your attention into the present.

Notice how your body feels, and what is going on in your mind. Simply letting go of whatever needs to be let go of so that you can be fully alert and present, right here, right now.

(Pause — spend around 5 minutes on the following seeing section.)

Now noticing what you can see, letting your eyes move around ... There is no need to keep them fixed anywhere. In fact, if you find your eyes fixating on any particular thing, notice this as a habit of the mind, a tendency of the attention to fix on things, and just letting it keep moving ...

Seeing the forms around you, the shapes and objects. Not just looking, but really *seeing* ...

Not getting involved in labelling them or thinking about them ... instead, just noticing the different shapes and colours, the different angles ... really seeing what is in front of you ...

(Pause)

And, of course, any time you realise that you have hopped on a train of thought, even if you have gone a few stations down the line, just getting back off again ... coming back to *this* moment ...

Just looking ...

(Pause)

And now, blurring your vision a bit so you are looking with soft eyes ... starting to notice shadow, noticing how everything you were just looking at casts a shadow ... you may not have been so aware of that until just now, but start to observe shadow instead of form ... as you do this, you are training your attention to notice things that usually go unnoticed. Just keep looking around and noticing how different shadows are everywhere ...

How every form casts a shadow, and these two are inextricably linked ... like how when it is day on one half of the world it is night on the other, and when it is summer in one hemisphere it is winter in the other, at the same time ...

(Pause)

At times you may find your attention goes back to seeing form ... Just noticing this tendency — it is one of the strong habits of the mind — and once again letting go of the forms and going back to seeing shadow ...

(Pause)

If you are outside and started off looking at trees, noticing now whether you were tuned in to the branches or the leaves ... if the branches, now start noticing the leaves ... if the leaves, bringing your attention to the branches ...

Wherever you are, start noticing what you weren't aware of when you began — shadow, new objects, whatever ...

Not trying too hard — just letting your eyes move around and being *curious* about what is there to be seen ... remembering that curiosity is one of the most important parts of mindfulness, along with awareness, and acceptance of what is happening ... bringing curiosity to your experience helps you to notice and learn new things. This is why little kids are such quick learners — they are naturally curious about everything ... but curiosity is something that you can practise, too, and will get better at as you keep training it ...

Now starting to look more with your peripheral vision ... rather than staring at things right in front of you, where they are crisp and sharp, blurring your vision a little and seeing what is there right at the edge of your visual field, right in the periphery ... you can't actually look right at it, or you will be staring again, but you can start to develop a kind of *awareness* of it ...

Seeing the space between objects ...

Bringing your mind back any time it wanders, remembering not to fight with your thoughts …

(Pause — spend about 5 minutes on the following hearing section, more if you like!)

And now, while you continue looking with a soft, wide gaze, also starting to hear the sounds around you … again, noticing those that grab your attention and also those that are off in the background — the soft sounds, the distant ones, the ones you weren't even aware of a few moments ago …

If you catch yourself fixing your attention on any one sound, just letting go and coming back to listening … simply listening, hearing all sounds, noticing the soundscape around you …

(Pause)

And now also noticing the silence in which sounds happen, the spaces between sounds … the silence out of which they emerge, and into which they disappear again …

(Pause)

So now just sitting and seeing with this wider vision, noticing shapes and shadows and the spaces between shapes and the spaces between shadows … and also listening to the sounds — from nearby and off in the distance … and also hearing the silence between sounds, in which the sounds happen …

Sitting in a spacious awareness, just being aware of each moment, moment to moment to moment …

Just relaxing your attention any time it gets tense and fixes on anything, and bringing back your wandering mind over and over, as many times as you need to …

And now just sitting … completely open, listening, seeing, just being present … notice what it's like to be really awake, really alert …

(Pause)

And now, as we bring the exercise to a close, hold this awareness as best you can as you go and do whatever you decide to do next … remembering to keep coming back to this wide awareness as often as you like.

Exercise 5: Mindful eating

For this exercise, you will need two sultanas or some other kind of food such as chocolate or fruit. The following text assumes you are eating a sultana, but you can adapt it to any food you like. The whole exercise should go for 5 minutes. Spend as long as you like on each part, and try to experience the act of eating the sultana as fully as you can. It can be good to then eat a second sultana in the same way (but perhaps without guiding the experience) so you can have an even richer experience.

Script

For this exercise, set aside anything you think you know about this food. Simply let go of any concepts or ideas you have and, as best you can, bring a fresh, curious awareness to it. It may even help to imagine that you are from another planet and have never seen this particular food before in your whole life.

Taking one of these objects and holding it in the palm of your hand, or between your finger and thumb …

Paying attention to seeing it ...

Looking at it carefully, as if you have never seen such a thing before ...

Turning it over between your fingers ...

Exploring its texture between your fingers ...

Noticing the raised edges and how they catch the light, and the darker hollows and valleys ... noticing its irregular shape, the way the light can pass through some parts better than others, the different colours ...

Noticing the small indentation on one end that is rather like a human navel, and perhaps reflecting on the fact that this object was once connected to a greater whole, drawing nutrients from the earth and the environment generally ...

Letting your eyes explore every part of it, as if you have never seen such a thing before ...

And if, while you are doing this, any thoughts come to mind like, 'What is the point of this?' or 'I don't like sultanas', then just noting these as thoughts and bringing your awareness back to the object ...

And now smelling the object, taking it and holding it under your nose ... noticing what happens in your mind as you do this ... lots of people find that they suddenly connect with memories, which reflects the fact that smell is the oldest and most primal sense we have, and connections go straight from the nose to the brain, unlike the other senses ...

If you notice any associations or memories appear in your mind, just acknowledge these and then come back to the actual smell of the object …

And now taking another look at it …

Consciously make the decision to, in a moment, place the sultana in your mouth … tune in to your body and notice what happens as you start to think about doing this … pay particular attention to your mouth and your stomach … notice how your body has already connected mentally with the experience of eating this sultana, and has already started to prepare itself physically …

And now slowly bringing the object to your mouth, noticing how your hand knows exactly where to put it, without any conscious thought … Actually, what you are observing here is the automatic pilot of eating, the fact that so much of our eating is done with very little conscious awareness …

And then gently placing the object in the mouth, noticing how it is 'received', without biting it, just exploring the sensations of having it in your mouth … perhaps noticing the automatic urge to start chewing — but just sitting with this urge for a moment longer, without indulging it, perhaps learning something about it as you do so …

And when you are ready, very consciously and deliberately biting into the object and starting to chew it …

Noticing the release of flavour, and seeing if you can tune in to *where* on your tongue you taste the sweet, the sour, and perhaps the saltiness and bitterness …

Noticing which teeth are doing the chewing ... are these the same teeth you always chew sultanas with? Feeling the activation of the jaw muscles and tuning right in to the experience of chewing ...

Noticing the urge to swallow and again just sitting with this urge without immediately indulging it ... noticing the automaticity of swallowing, and perhaps reflecting for a moment on how often you would just do this without much conscious awareness ...

Then, when you feel ready to swallow, doing this with as much awareness as possible ... noticing the movement of the tongue and seeing if you can stay in touch with the sultana as it moves down your throat and right down into your stomach ...

Becoming aware that the sultana is now part of your body, at least for the next little while ... Some mindfulness teachers like to jokingly suggest at this point that you may even like to become aware that you are now exactly one sultana heavier.

Exercise 6a: Mindful walking

This practice brings mindfulness to movement, which is important for two main reasons. First, it emphasises the fact that mindfulness is about being aware and awake in each moment, rather than being specifically about sitting meditation. Second, we spend much of the day walking and moving about, and so learning to do this mindfully is a way of bringing mindfulness more fully into our daily life.

Script

Stand relaxed with your eyes closed or half closed. Make sure that you can walk in a small circle or for a few metres straight in front of you, and ensure there are no obstacles in your path.

Tune in to your body. Notice how it feels to stand. Feel the weight distribution on your feet. Notice which muscles are involved in holding you up. Let go of tension in any other muscles. Observe where the breath naturally fills the body on the inhalation. Let go of any tension in the chest or abdomen so that your body breathes unimpeded. Really feel what it is like to stand, relaxed and alert.

Very slowly and deliberately, take a step. Really tune in to the movement, feeling as much as you can about it. Feel the weight transfer onto the other leg and foot. Feel your momentum move you forward. Feel the weight come out of the leg and the heel begin to lift up. Then the ball of the foot as it breaks contact with the ground. Then feel your body balance automatically as your leg and foot travel through the air. Then feel your heel make contact with the ground in front of you, and feel the weight transfer back into that leg and foot, and then out of the other one.

At the same time, tune in to the muscles. Feel them activate as they become involved in the movement, and then deactivate as they are no longer required. See if you can become aware of excess muscle activation — or even tension. We often habitually use too much force, and engage muscles that aren't needed (e.g. notice what is happening right now in your face and your hands).

Keep walking in this way in a circle (or for as many paces straight in front as you can, then turn and walk back in the same mindful way).

Stay connected to your breath while doing this. Keep breathing.

After some time you might like to speed up the walk, but make sure you remain mindful and don't snap back into reflexive habits of unconscious walking.

You might like to practise walking to the bus stop like this, or from your desk to the bathroom. Keep reconnecting with the simple act of walking throughout the day. If you are late for your bus or train, experiment with walking fast yet staying relaxed and keeping your attention in your body (rather than imagining the train pulling away as you get to the station, or your teacher's or boss' face as you arrive late). Notice how walking like this changes the experience.

Exercise 6b: Mindful stretching

This is another way to get more fully into your body and therefore bring mindfulness more fully into your daily life. It is a very useful approach, generally, to bring to *any* form of exercise, and once you have familiarised yourself with this exercise you could start being more mindful as you work out in the gym, do yoga or martial arts, or even just as you reach for your stapler.

Script

Think of your five favourite stretches (in yoga, such poses are called asanas).

Start as in the mindful walking exercise by tuning in to your body. Really take some time to get in touch with what it feels like to sit/stand/lie and breathe.

Then, very mindfully and deliberately, move into the stretch or pose. Really pay attention as you *move into* it, rather than just suddenly finding yourself *in* it. Feel the weight transfer and muscle activation/deactivation, as in the last exercise (read through it if you haven't already).

Pause at the limits of the stretch, at the point where it becomes uncomfortable. Practise being kind to your body, rather than forcing it to do things it isn't ready for. But at the same time, gently explore what it is like to go beyond your limits. Remain for a time at the point where tension starts to enter the body. Breathe with the tension and relax around it, making sure you don't try to get rid of it or force your way through it. Then, when you have accepted it and softened around it, go a little further into the stretch.

Move *out* of each pose in the same mindful way. Make sure that you use *each* moment of the stretch to learn about your body and to practise mindfulness.

Keep breathing throughout the stretches.

To take this mindfulness 'off the mat' and out into your day, stay as connected as possible to your posture and body generally. Notice how you are standing and moving throughout the day, and try to use as little effort as possible. When you reach for something (e.g. a stapler or pen), do it with as little muscle activation as possible. Perhaps you need to move your feet to stand a little closer (or further away) so the movement can be natural.

Exercise 7: Stress response

Practising mindfulness is no guarantee against having experiences of anxiety or stress. In fact, early in the development of mindfulness skills, it is likely that a person with a background level of stress or anxiety will become more aware of its presence. That is not a problem but rather a sign of progress and an opportunity to learn to work with it in a more skillful way.

The guidance in this exercise is to supplement any of the previous practices such as the body scan or breathing where you feel that anxiety is an issue or it has come up in discussion as a problem for one or more members of the group.

The main issue here is for the students practising to be reminded that they don't have to block out the anxiety or to make it go away if it arises. Our experience will have taught us that this only fixates the attention on the anxiety, making it more intrusive. In fact, there is no need to resist it at all, and the person is not doing something wrong if it comes up during the practice. On the contrary, the person practising can welcome anxiety as an opportunity to learn to work with it (i.e. not to react, elaborate or judge it). Each time it arises just let the thoughts, feelings and bodily sensations ebb and flow as they will, just observing them with less and less involvement each time, almost like riding a wave instead of resisting it. The issue is not the presence of anxiety, but rather our attitude towards it.

At the completion of the practice invite the students to reflect on their experience and facilitate the conversation in an open, impartial and non-judgmental way. There is no right or wrong experience. For example, what arose during the practice? If stress or anxiety arose, what was the attitude or reaction to it? What effect did that have on the experience of the stress or anxiety? Where did the attention go? What lesson does that teach us? What is the most useful attitude to cultivate to such experiences if they arise?

Exercise 8: Working mindfully with emotions

In this exercise we use mindfulness to simply let negative emotions be there, without getting overwhelmed by them or getting into a tug of war with them. This is particularly useful in the lead-up to and during a performance. You may have noticed how when you try to repress your emotions they sometimes get even stronger because the attention fixates on them. The same happens when you go with them and give them energy. An alternative is to simply let them be there, come and go, and keep yourself centred in the present using your body and breath.

Script

Start by sitting comfortably and noticing your whole body ...

First of all, just feel your body ... becoming aware of the state it is in right now ... observing whether it is tired ... or alert ... or relaxed ... heavy or light ... whether you can feel it clearly or whether it is hard to feel ... just noticing how it *is* right now ...

Let go of any tension that you find anywhere ...

And just let your body settle into whatever position it is in ... sitting or lying ...

And also becoming aware of your mind. What thoughts are around? Is your mind calm and present ... or dull and sleepy ... or agitated and scattered? ...

Whatever you notice, in your body and your mind, just letting it be there exactly as it is ... not fighting with it ... not trying to change it ... not thinking about it ... just letting it be there ... bringing an attitude of acceptance and friendliness to it ...

And then noticing how it feels to breathe ... feeling the expansion and contraction of your belly ... the rise and fall of your shoulders ... maybe you can even feel the air brushing in and out of your nostrils ...

Taking a few deeper breaths ...

And then just letting your breathing settle into its own rhythm ... letting your body breathe naturally, as it knows how to do and as it does even when you are not paying any attention to it ...

Just noticing how it feels to breathe in ... and out ...

(Pause)

Letting go of any tension on the out-breath …

Resting your attention lightly on the breath … not blocking anything out … or getting too fixed on the breath … just using it as an anchor to keep your attention in the present …

Following each breath all the way through — start, middle and end …

Noticing the point where it turns around …

Being really *curious* how it feels to breathe …

And any time your attention wanders off — no matter where it goes — simply noticing where it has gone, then gently escorting it back to the breath …

And just as with the body scan, bringing it back over and over and over again, as many times as you need to …

Seeing how quickly you can catch your attention when it sneaks off …

(Pause)

Just being aware when you're breathing in … and when you're breathing out …

Letting go of any tension in your belly … so that your body can just breathe naturally … without any resistance …

(Pause)

Don't worry if it feels like you are controlling your breath a little — this is natural … just noticing this thought — it's just a thought — and continue noticing what it feels like as you breathe in … and out … in … and out …

Just coming back to the breath any time your attention wanders off …

Letting thoughts and feelings just go through to the keeper … keeping your eye on your breath … just feeling it coming and going, from moment to moment …

(Longer pause)

Now notice any emotions that are around … any feelings …

Perhaps there are obvious ones that have been there for a while …

Or perhaps you will need to consciously get in touch with some … to do this, think of a difficult situation, where you were really anxious or annoyed or sad … and where you had trouble shaking the feeling … really remembering the situation … what you were thinking … what you felt … stepping right into the memory … really being back there …

(Pause)

Now just noticing how the emotion feels in your body … noticing where in your body you feel it most strongly … taking your mind there and getting curious about how it actually feels …

Drop the story that goes along with it … just notice the thoughts — the words and images and everything else that is happening in your brain — and let them be there without resisting them or getting into them …

228

Instead, just focusing on what you can feel ... really noticing *where* in your body you feel it ... noticing the intensity of the sensations ... and any other sensory qualities — weight ... density ... temperature ... movement ... a sense of expansion or contraction ...

Just feeling whatever is actually there to be felt ...

And now, starting to breathe with the sensations ... breathing into them and out of them ... imagining that your breath goes right into them on an inhale, and out from them on an exhale ... not doing this to get rid of the sensations or change them ... just making space for them to be there as they are ...

Dropping the story any time it comes back ... and just feeling the sensations from moment to moment, breath to breath ...

(Pause)

Getting really *curious* about how the sensations feel as you breathe *in* and as you breathe *out* ...

Curiosity is the key here ... in any moment where you are really curious, *really* noticing how something is ... in that moment you are not *reacting* to it ... but are just observing it ... accepting it as it is ...

So really feeling the sensations as you breathe in ... and out ... in ... and out ...

(Pause)

What do you notice? ... Perhaps if you really pay attention you may notice that the sensations change a little as you breathe in and out ... that they feel slightly different on the in-breath compared to the out-breath ...

(Pause)

Perhaps they don't seem to be changing in any way ... but as you breathe into them and out of them and keep letting go of the story and any judgments, that the sensations can just be there as they are ... and you can just breathe with them ...

Or perhaps at times you get overwhelmed by the feelings or get totally caught up in the story ... if this happens, just keep coming back to the breath ... even opening your eyes if you need to ...

And maybe the sensations have actually gone already ... if this is the case, you can either keep focusing on the sensations throughout your body and just wait until the next emotion comes up ... or you can consciously remember the situation again to get the feelings back ...

Whatever is happening for you, just noticing that ... and keep coming back to the sensations ... breathing with them ... letting them be there just as they are ...

Or keeping your attention on your body ... simply feeling what is there to be felt ... noticing your breath as it shows up from moment to moment, breath to breath ...

(Longer pause)

And as we start bringing this exercise to a close, just taking a moment to notice what it has been like to work with your emotions in this way ...

Did you learn anything new? Did you find there was some benefit to being willing to *feel* your emotions in this way? Or maybe you need to practise this a few times to really get what it gives you ...

And when you are ready, opening your eyes and bringing your attention back more fully to where you are.

Exercise 9: Communicating with awareness

The guidelines provided in Chapter 11 should be enough to start communicating with more awareness and intentionality. The exercise included here is simply a way of formally training these mindful communication skills, developing them in a more structured way.

This is an interpersonal mindfulness practice, so you will need another person to do this with. Decide who will be the mindful speaker and listener — you will get a chance to swap over afterward.

Start by sitting across from your partner at a comfortable distance. Close your eyes and tune in to your body and your breath. Notice how your awareness of the person sitting across from you affects you. Let go of any tension in the body and let any thoughts and feelings go by without engaging with them.

Then open your eyes and look at your partner. Again, notice how this affects your body and mind. Settle in to the experience of connecting with the person across from you, letting go of any tension and any thoughts.

Mindful speaking

The speaker starts by mindfully saying something. This can be as simple as describing what you are feeling in your body in that moment, or it could be a description of the last holiday you went on, what you did on the weekend, and so on. It just needs to be something you can talk about.

As you do so, you should take moments to pause and reflect on what you *actually* want to say. There is a very strong automatic pilot that shows up sometimes when we are talking — we can get in to a track and start to chatter mindlessly. Taking moments to pause and feel into your body (perhaps even closing your eyes to really tune in to yourself) helps you avoid this tendency.

The goal of the speaker is just to speak in this more mindful way. The content of what you say is not what is important. What is being practised here is the ability to speak mindfully — speaking your truth, from your heart, as best you can. And after saying something, taking a moment to reflect on whether that is actually what you wanted to say, and whether it came out the way you intended. You may also like to pay attention to what you observe in your partner as you speak, getting instant feedback about how they might be receiving the message.

Mindful listening

At the same time as the speaker is speaking mindfully, the listener is practising fully listening to what is being said. This goes far beyond the actual words being spoken. As discussed earlier, around 80 per cent of communication is non-verbal — including things like rate, pitch and tone of voice, body language and eye gaze. So the job of the listener is to *really* listen. Not just hear, but to listen fully to the full picture of what the speaker is saying, with their whole being.

Obviously this will require noticing when the attention wanders off into judgment or mind-wandering, and bringing it back. It will also require noticing the tendency to think about what you want to say in response, and letting go of this.

Treat this practice like an exercise for noticing these tendencies and developing the ability to fully listen despite them. We recommend that each round of listening/speaking goes for at least 3 or 4 minutes, to give each person time to really get into the exercise, noticing the habits of unmindful communication and developing the capacity to really connect.

If looking into your partner's eyes becomes too confronting at any point, feel free to avert your gaze. Perhaps watch their breathing for a while.

Maybe even try breathing with them, and observe what this does to the level of your connection.

Debrief and practical application

After doing this exercise for some time, perhaps after each round, spend some time sharing with your partner what the experience was like. It can be very interesting to hear how other people experience your own communication. They will probably notice things that you had no idea about.

And after you have finished the exercise, pay more attention to the way you communicate generally. As best you can, stay connected to your body as you speak, and whenever anyone speaks to you tune in to the whole communication — the verbal and non-verbal aspects. Investigate how listening and speaking in this way improve your communication and relationships with the people around you.

Exercise 10: Music

Music of various types can have significant effects on emotions, behaviours and states of attention. This exercise is framed as an experiment in noticing the effects of music generally and different types of music in particular.

You will need a sound system of at least reasonable quality. You might like to do this exercise with just one piece of music or you may wish to have three or four pieces of music ready if you wish the group to reflect on the effects of different types of music. The aim is not so much to praise or condemn any particular type of music but for the students to be more aware of the impact of music on the state of mind (thoughts and emotions), body, behaviour and attention. Invite them to notice this as they listen to each piece of music.

This exercise can be practised sitting up or lying down. If lying down ensure that the students are comfortable and have enough space around them that they are not infringing on other students' space. When settled in position, take the students through a brief body scan for a couple of minutes, preferably with the eyes closed. Then invite the students to engage their attention with the sense of hearing. For the first 15 to 30 seconds let the hearing be of the ambient sounds before starting the music. It would be helpful to ensure that the volume is clearly audible but also soft enough that the students do not get a shock when the music begins. Throughout the listening period the students are asked to let the music be the focus of attention, not having to block out anything else, but simply to notice when the attention wanders from the music and to gently re-engage the attention with it. It is also helpful for students to be aware of their preconceived ideas about musical likes and dislikes and to let those go, otherwise they won't be listening to the music so much as to an internal dialogue about the music. They are simply invited to listen to this music now, on its merits, noticing its effect in a non-judgmental way.

After the music is completed invite the students to share their reflections on what they noticed about their minds, bodies and attention and if the music did or did not give rise to peace, calm or clarity or, conversely, to any particular emotion, impulse or behaviour.

The choice of what music to listen to will be important as far as being more or less conducive to cultivating one or other state of mind, body, behaviour or attention. For example, a slower movement of Mozart or Bach, an ancient chant or shakuhachi flute might have a settling or relaxing effect. If you play some pop or dance music then there might be a different effect. A folk song or traditional ethnic music might have other effects, especially if it is evocative of happy or sad emotions. If playing a number of pieces then you may wish to start with the most busy or fast paced and finish with the quieter or more settling piece. It would be useful to put 15 to 30 seconds of space (ambient sounds) between each piece and at the end before completing the experiment.

At the end of the exercise invite the students to share their experiences and reflect on which music they would choose to get them moving, to focus, to settle or to relax.

Exercise 11a: Multitasking — communicating

This exercise is a good experiment for exploring the impact of multitasking on performance and depth of experience with particular reference to an important function: our capacity to communicate effectively.

In this exercise ask the students in the class to pair up, making sure that at least one member of each pair has a mobile device with them. Ask each pair to sit facing each other and for one of the pair to be prepared to speak to their partner about something they are authentically passionate about in their life — it could be a hobby, a person, a pet, their work, travel, their love of food or anything else. Ask the other member of each pair to attempt to listen to the person speaking about their passion but at the same time to be on their mobile device either texting or going through emails. The person who is on their mobile device is required to continue multitasking throughout the whole period of communication, (i.e. to continue to have their attention on the device at the same time as attempting to listen to their partner).

When each pair has decided who is going to take which role, ask the group to commence the multitasking communication exercise. Let the conversation run for about 3 minutes and then ask the group to stop. Spend the next few minutes asking the group what their experience was like of being either the person speaking to someone who was multitasking, or the one multitasking while listening. For example, what effect did it have on following content, comprehension, memory or clarity of communication? What was the effect on the depth of communication, or the emotional experience of speaking or listening? Was the person speaking feeling passionate about their chosen topic or was the person listening sharing the passion with any depth? What effect did it have on the level of engagement or connectedness during the conversation?

Now ask the group to reverse roles but this time the one listening will not be multitasking; rather, they will be giving the person speaking their full and undivided attention. Just as in mindfulness meditation, if the mind wanders off the listener will practise noticing where the attention has gone and gently bring it back to the person speaking. After 3 minutes of speaking, debrief the exercise again with questions such as the ones above and compare the experience of mindful listening with the multitasking one. Which was more fulfilling? Which was preferable? Why?

Exercise 11b: Multitasking — problem solving

This exercise can be a good one for participants to get some insight into the effect of multitasking on problem solving, which is an aspect of reasoning or executive functioning. Begin by choosing a problem-solving task such as:

- working on a piece of class work (for example, a maths or physics problem, creative writing, or writing an assignment)
- a problem like a Sudoku or a puzzle.

Make sure everyone has their work at the ready, then ask them to commence work together, but in the first instance ask them to multitask by working on the chosen activity while on social media at the same time. Give them at least 5 minutes of multitasking. Then ask the participants to stop work and debrief. Inquire into how effectively or quickly they worked, what effect multitasking had on problem-solving ability or creativity and how it affected their enjoyment of the task.

Next invite the students to work on a similar but different problem (for example, another Sudoku or puzzle of a similar degree of difficulty) or to continue with the same piece of class work but this time without multitasking. Invite the students to give their full and undivided attention to the task, including observing and non-judgmentally letting go of thoughts about and reactions to the task if they arise. Give a similar amount of time to participants as you gave in the first part of the exercise. Once again, ask the participants to stop and debrief.

Invite the participants to compare experiences and reflect on which was more effective, time efficient and creative. Was there a difference in problem-solving ability?

Some may well say they enjoyed the first experience more when they were on social media at the same time, but this is a reflection of their desire or compulsion to be on social media and not a reflection on their enjoyment or capacity to work or study.

Exercise 12: Working with distractions

One of the things that is most often a source of frustration for people learning mindfulness is the belief that one needs to block out 'distractions' whether they be things going on in the environment such as sounds, or things going on within us such as thoughts or sensations. The extent to which our attention is drawn to or influenced by such things is called 'distracter influence'. It is an issue not just during mindfulness meditation but also at other times, for example while trying to study with noise coming from the next room or worry about an upcoming exam.

Experience soon teaches us that the attempt to block things out only makes them more intrusive. A 'distraction' is just something happening, like anything else, but which we have decided shouldn't be there. We therefore turn 'something happening' from something neutral into a distraction and probably a stressor. The effect this has on attention is for us to subtly monitor to see if the thing is still there and whether we have blocked it out yet. This then causes the 'distraction' to become even more intrusive because we have turned it into a magnet for the attention, making it harder for the attention to rest on whatever we intend it to rest on, for example the breath or our assignment. The solution? Let's not put any pressure on ourselves to block anything out or to make distractions go away. In fact, let's not even label anything as a distraction in the first place.

In this exercise, invite the group to acknowledge the presence of something obvious and persistent in the environment. It could be the airconditioning, the traffic noise or anything else you choose. Then ask the group to practise a brief period of mindfulness meditation but instruct them at the outset to attempt to totally block out the nominated sound so that they can't hear it at all. After about 20 seconds, while still practising, ask them to note whether they are being successful in totally blocking out the sound. If they can still hear it then suggest that they try even harder to block it out. After another 20 seconds ask the group to stop the practice and report back on their experience.

Most will note that the 'distraction' became more obvious and dominated their attention the harder they tried to make it go away. This might have also been associated with frustration. There may be a few who noted that they weren't distracted by it, not because they blocked it out but because they rested their attention on something else to the point that they stopped noticing the distraction.

The lesson really is not about trying to block out anything during mindfulness practice, but just to note that at any given moment there are thousands of things we could pay attention to but we just happen to nominate or prefer one thing in particular rather than something else. It's more a matter of choosing what to be interested in so that the attention engages with that, and learning not to be interested in something else. We don't have to block it out; it will recede by itself.

ENDNOTES

Introduction

1. *Shorter Oxford English Dictionary on Historical Principles*, Oxford Third Edition, Clarendon Press, 1992, p. 630.

Chapter 1

1. William James, *The Principles of Psychology*, (1890), Dover Publications, 1950.

Chapter 2

1. Pascual-Leone, A., Amedi, A., Fregni, F., and Merabet, L.B., 'The plastic human brain cortex', *Annual Review of Neuroscience*, 2005;28:377–401.

2. Pascual-Leone, A., 'The brain that plays music and is changed by it', *Annals of the New York Academy of Sciences*, 2001;930(1):315–29.

3. Zhao, X.H., Wang, P.J., Li, C.B., Hu, Z.H., Xi, Q., Wu, W.Y. and Tang, X.W., 'Altered default mode network activity in patient with anxiety disorders: An fMRI study', *European Journal of Radiology*, 2007;63(3):373–8.

4. Greicius, M.D., Flores, B.H., Menon, V., Glover, G.H., Solvason, H.B., Kenna, H. and Schatzberg, A.F., 'Resting-state functional connectivity in major depression: Abnormally increased contributions from subgenual cingulate cortex and thalamus', *Biological Psychiatry*, 2007;62(5):429–37.

5. Uddin, L.Q., Kelly, A.M.C., Biswal, B.B., Margulies, D.S., Shehzad, Z., Shaw, D., Ghaffari, M., Rotrosen, J., Adler, L.A., Castellanos, F.X. and Milham, M.P., 'Network homogeneity reveals decreased integrity of default-mode network in ADHD', *Journal of Neuroscience Methods*, 2008a;169:249–54.

6. Firbank, M.J., Blamire, A.M., Krishnan, M.S., Teodorczuk, A., English, P., Gholkar, A. and O'Brien, J.T., 'Atrophy is associated with posterior cingulate white matter disruption in dementia with Lewy bodies and Alzheimer's disease', *Neuroimage*, 2007;36(1):1.

7. Pomarol-Clotet, E., Salvador, R., Sarro, S., Gomar, J.,Vila, F., Martinez, A. and McKenna, P.J., 'Failure to deactivate in the prefrontal cortex in schizophrenia: Dysfunction of the default mode network?', *Psychological Medicine*, 2008;38(8):1185–94.

8. Kennedy, D.P. and Courchesne, E., 'Functional abnormalities of the default network during self- and other-reflection in autism', *Social Cognitive and Affective Neuroscience*, 2008;3(2):177–90.

9. Chambers, R., Lo, B.C.Y. and Allen, N.B., 'The impact of intensive mindfulness training on attentional control, cognitive style, and affect', *Cognitive Therapy and Research*, 2008;32(3):303–22.

10. Ramsburg, Jared T. and Youmans, Robert J., 'Meditation in the higher-education classroom: Meditation improves student knowledge retention during lectures, *Mindfulness*, 2013;DOI:10.1007/s12671-013-0199-5.

11. Nass et al. in Dretzin, Rachel. and Rushkoff, Douglas, 'Digital nation — life on the virtual frontier', www.pbs.org, *Frontline*, February 2010, accessed 14 April 2011.

12. Hofmann, S.G., Sawyer, A.T., Witt, A.A. and Oh, D., 'The effect of mindfulness-based therapy on anxiety and depression: A meta-analytic review', *Journal of Consulting and Clinical Psychology*, 2010;78(2):169–83.

13. Epel, E., Daubenmier, J., Moskowitz, J.T., Folkman, S. and Blackburn, E., 'Can meditation slow rate of cellular aging? Cognitive stress, mindfulness, and telomeres', *Annals of the New York Academy of Sciences*, 2009;1172(1):34–53.

14. Chambers, R.H., Gullone, E., Hassed, C., Knight, W., Garvin, T. and Allen, N.B., 'Mindful emotion regulation predicts recovery in depressed youth' (currently submitted to *Mindfulness*).

Chapter 3

1. Adapted from Biggs, John, 1987, *Student Approaches to Learning and Studying*, Australian Council for Educational Research, Melbourne.

2. Bullimore, D., 1998, *Study Skills and Tomorrow's Doctors*, W.B. Saunders, Edinburgh.

3. Hassed C., 2002, *Know Thyself: The stress release program*, Hill of Content, Melbourne.

4. Flook L., Goldberg S.B., Pinger L., Bonus K. and Davidson R.J., 'Mindfulness for teachers: A pilot study to assess effects on stress, burnout, and teaching efficacy', *Mind, Brain, and Education*, 2013;7(3):182–195. ePub 16 August 2013. DOI: 10.1111/mbe.12026.

5. Klingberg T., Forssberg H. and Westerberg H., 'Training of working memory in children with ADHD', *Journal of Clinical & Experimental Neuropsychology*, 2002;24:781–91.

6. Ashcraft M.H., Kirk E.P., 'The relationships among working memory, math anxiety, and performance', *Journal of Experimental Psychology: General*, June 2001;130(2):224–37.

7. Beilock, S.L. and Carr, T.H., 'When high-powered people fail: Working memory and "choking under pressure" in math', *Psychological Science*, 2005;16(2):101–5.

Chapter 6

1. Bond, K., Ospina, M.B., Hooton, N., Bialy, L., Dryden, D.M., Buscemi, N., David Shannahoff-Khalsa, D., Jeffrey Dusek, J. and Carlson, L.E., 'Defining a complex intervention: The development of demarcation criteria for "meditation"', *Psychology of Religion and Spirituality*, American Psychological Association, 2009;1(2):129–37, DOI:10.1037/a0015736.

2 Lutz, Antoine, L. et al. 'Attention regulation and monitoring in meditation', *Trends in Cognitive Sciences*, 2008;12(4):163–9.

3. Readers interested in knowing more about these two broad types of meditation — and the variety of examples of each — are referred to *The Meditative Mind: The varieties of the meditative experience* by Daniel Goleman, New York, Penguin, 1988.

4. Miller, G.A., 'The magical number seven, plus or minus two: Some limits on our capacity for processing information', *Psychological Review*, 1956;63 (2):81–97.

5. Klingberg, T., Forssberg, H. and Westerberg, H., 'Training of working memory in children with ADHD', *Journal of Clinical and Experimental Neuropsychology*, 2002;24(6):781–91.

6. Jha, A.P., Stanley, E.A., Kiyonaga, A., Wong, L. and Gelfand, L., 'Examining the protective effects of mindfulness training on working memory capacity and affective experience', *Emotion*, 2010;10(1):54.

7. Hölzel, B.K., Carmody, J., Vangel, M. et al., 'Mindfulness practice leads to increases in regional brain gray matter density', *Psychiatry Research*, 30 January 2011;191(1):36–43.

8. Slagter, H.A., Lutz, A., Greischar, L.L., Francis, A.D., Nieuwenhuis, S., Davis, J.M. and Davidson, R.J., 'Mental training affects distribution of limited brain resources', *PLOS Biology*, 2007;5(6):e138.

Chapter 7

1. Tian, F., Tu, S., Qiu, J. et al., 'Neural correlates of mental preparation for successful insight problem solving', *Behavioural Brain Research*, 20 January 2011;216(2):626–30, DOI:10.1016/j.bbr.2010.09.005. ePub 15 September 2010.

2, Sibinga, E.M. and Wu, A.W., 'Clinician mindfulness and patient safety', *Journal of the American Medical Association*, 2010;304(22):2532–3.

3. Greenberg, J., Reiner, K. and Meiran, N., '"Mind the trap": Mindfulness practice reduces cognitive rigidity', *PLOS One*, 2012;7(5):e36206. ePub 15 May 2012.

4. http://www.talbenshahar.com/

5. Zeidan, F., Johnson, S.K., Diamond, B.J., David, Z. and Goolkasian, P., 'Mindfulness meditation improves cognition: Evidence of brief mental training', *Consciousness and Cognition*, June 2010;19(2):597–605. ePub 3 April 2010.

Chapter 8

1. Dweck, C.S., *Mindset: The new psychology of success*, Random House, New York, 2006.
2. http://mindsetonline.com/
3. Kamins, M. and Dweck, C.S., 'Person vs. process praise and criticism: Implications for contingent self-worth and coping', *Developmental Psychology*, 1999;35:835–47.
4. Cimpian, A., Arce, H., Markman, E.M. and Dweck, C.S., 'Subtle linguistic cues impact children's motivation', *Psychological Science*, 2007;18:314–16.
5. http://mindsetonline.com/changeyourmindset/firststeps/index.html

Chapter 9

1. Ashcraft, M.H. and Kirk, E.P., 'The relationships among working memory, math anxiety, and performance', *Journal of Experimental Psychology: General*, June 2001;130(2):224–37.
2. Beilock, S.L. and Carr, T.H., 'When high-powered people fail: Working memory and "choking under pressure" in math', *Psychological Science*, 2005;16(2):101–5.

Chapter 10

1. Larson, R.W. and Sheeber, L.B., 'The daily emotional experience of adolescents: Are adolescents more emotional, why, and how is that related to depression?', in Allen, N. and Sheeber, L. (eds), *Adolescent Emotional Development and the Emergence of Depressive Disorders*, Cambridge University Press, Cambridge, 2008.
2. Allen, N.B. and Sheeber, L.B., 'The importance of affective development for the emergence of depressive disorders during adolescence', in Allen, N. and Sheeber, L. (eds), *Adolescent Emotional Development and the Emergence of Depressive Disorders*, Cambridge University Press, Cambridge, 2008.
3. Brydon, L., Lin J., Butcher, L., Hamer, M., Erusalimsky, J.D., Blackburn, E.H. and Steptoe, A., 'Hostility and cellular aging in men from the Whitehall II cohort', *Biological Psychiatry*, 3 October 2011;71(9):767–73.
4. Gross, J.J. and John, O.P., 'Individual differences in two emotion regulation processes: Implications for affect, relationships, and well-being', *Journal of Personality and Social Psychology*, August 2003;85(2):348–62.
5. Chambers, R.H., Gullone, E., Allen, N.B., Hassed, C.S., Garvin, T. and Knight, W., 'Mindful emotion regulation predicts recovery in depressed youth', *Preparation*, 2013.
6. Kuyken, W., Weare, K. and Ukoumunne, O.C. et al., 'Effectiveness of the Mindfulness in Schools Programme: A non-randomised controlled feasibility study', *British Journal of Psychiatry*, 20 June 2013;1–6. DOI: 10.1192/bjp.bp.113.126649 (ePub ahead of print).

Chapter 11

1. Singer, T., Seymour, B., O'Doherty, J. et al., 'Empathy for pain involves the affective but not sensory components of pain', *Science*, 20 February 2004;303(5661):1157–62.

2. Baer, R.A., Smith, G.T. and Allen, K.B., 'Assessment of mindfulness by self-report: The Kentucky inventory of mindfulness skills', *Assessment*, 2004;11(3):191–206.

3. Lutz A., Brefczynski-Lewis J., Johnstone T., Davidson R.J., Regulation of the neural circuitry of emotion by compassion meditation: Effects of meditative expertise. *PLOS One*. 26 March 2008;3(3):e1897. DOI:10.1371/journal.pone.0001897.

4. Forero, R., McLellan, L., Rissel, C. and Bauman, A., 'Bullying behaviour and psychosocial health among school students in New South Wales, Australia: Cross sectional survey', *British Medical Journal*, 7 August 1999;319(7206):344–8.

5. Resnick, M.D., Bearman, P.S., Blum, R.W. et al., 'Protecting adolescents from harm. Findings from the National Longitudinal Study on Adolescent Health', *Journal of the American Medical Association*, 10 September 1997;278(10):823–32.

Chapter 12

1. Australian Communications and Media Authority, Communications Report 2008–2009.

2. Sanders, C.E., Field, T.M., Diego, M. and Kaplan, M., 'The relationship of Internet use to depression and social isolation among adolescents', *Adolescence*, 2000;35:237–42.

3. Angster, A., Frank, M. and Lester, D., 'An exploratory study of students' use of cell phones, texting, and social networking sites', *Psychological Reports*, 2010;107:402–04.

4. Lillard, A.S. and Peterson, J., 'The immediate impact of different types of television on young children's executive function', *Pediatrics*, accessed 12 September 2011, DOI: 10.1542/peds.2010–1919.

5. Swing, E.L., Gentile, D.A., Anderson, C.A. and Walsh, D.A., 'Television and video game exposure and the development of attention problems', *Pediatrics*, August 2010;126(2):214 21. DOI: 10.1542/peds.2009–1508. ePub 5 July 2010.

6. Landau, S.M., Marks, S.M., Mormino, E.C., Rabinovici, G.D., Oh, H., O'Neil, J.P., Wilson, R.S. and Jagust, W.J., 'Association of lifetime cognitive engagement and low -amyloid deposition', *Archives of Neurology*, ePub 23 January 2012.

7. Scarmeas, N., Levy, G., Tang, M.X., Manly, J. and Stern, Y., 'Influence of leisure activity on the incidence of Alzheimer's disease', *Neurology*, 2001;57(12):2236–42.

8. Friedland, R.P., Fritsch, T., Smyth, K.A., Koss, E., Lerner, A.J., Chen, C.H. and Debanne, S.M., 'Patients with Alzheimer's disease have reduced activities in midlife compared with healthy control-group members', *Proceedings of the National Academy of Sciences*, 2001;98(6):3440–5.

9. Van den Bulck, J., 'The effects of media on sleep', *Adolescent Medicine: State of the Art Reviews*, 2010;21:418–29.

10. Halayem, S., Nouira, O., Bourgou, S. et al., 'The mobile: A new addiction upon adolescents', *La Tunisie Médicale*, 2010;88:593–6.

11. Sansone, R.A. and Sansone, L.A., 'Cell phones: The psychosocial risks', *Innovations in Clinical Neuroscience*, 2013;10(1):33–7.

Chapter 13

1. Mitchell, J.H., Broeren, S., Newall, C. and Hudson, J.L., 'An experimental manipulation of maternal perfectionistic anxious rearing behaviors with anxious and non-anxious children', *Journal of Experimental Child Psychology*, 15 February 2013. DOI:pii: S0022 0965(12)00247–0. 10.1016/j.jecp.2012.12.006.

Chapter 14

1. Nelson, M.C. and Gordon-Larsen, P., 'Physical activity and sedentary behavior patterns are associated with selected adolescent health risk behaviors', *Pediatrics*, April 2006;117(4):1281–90.

2. Chaouloff, F., 'Effects of acute physical exercise on central serotonergic systems', *Medicine and Science in Sports and Exercise*, January 1997;29(1):58–62.

3. Cited in, Harung, H., Travis, F., Blank, W. and Heaton, D., 'Higher development, brain integration, and excellence in leadership', *Management Decision*, 47(6):872–94.

4. Young, J.A. and Pain, M.D., 'The Zone: Evidence of a universal phenomenon for athletes across sports', *Athletic Insight*, 1999;1(3):21–30.

5. Csíkzentmihályi, M., *Flow: The psychology of optimal experience*, Harper & Rowe, New York, 1990.

6. Summarised in McKenzie, S. and Hassed, C., *Mindfulness for Life*, Exisle, Wollombi, NSW, 2012.

Chapter 15

1. Hallowell, E.M., 'Overloaded circuits: Why smart people underperform', *Harvard Business Review*, January 2005;83(1):54–62,116.

2. Cancelliere, C., Cassidy, J.D., Ammendolia, C. and Côté, P., 'Are workplace health promotion programs effective at improving presenteeism in workers? A systematic review and best evidence synthesis of the literature', *BMC Public Health*, 26 May 2011;11:395. DOI: 10.1186/1471–2458–11–395.

3. Swing, E.L., Gentile, D.A., Anderson, C.A. and Walsh, D.A., 'Television and video game exposure and the development of attention problems', *Pediatrics*, August 2010;126(2):214

21. DOI: 10.1542/peds.2009–1508.

4. Lillard, A.S. and Peterson, J., 'The immediate impact of different types of television on young children's executive function', *Pediatrics*, accessed 12 September 2011. DOI: 10.1542/peds.2010–1919.5. Halayem, S., Nouira, O., Bourgou, S. et al., 'The mobile: A new addiction upon adolescents', *La Tunisie Médicale*, 2010;88:593–6.

6. Seibel, F.L. and Johnson, W.B., 'Parental control, trait anxiety, and satisfaction with life in college students', *Psychology Reports*, April 2001;88(2):473–80.

7. Purdie, N., Carroll, A. and Roche, L., 'Parenting and adolescent self-regulation', *Journal of Adolescence*, December 2004;27(6):663–76.

8. Heaven, P.C. and Ciarrochi, J., Parental styles, conscientiousness, and academic performance in high school: A three-wave longitudinal study', *Personality and Social Psychology Bulletin*, April 2008;34(4):451–61. DOI: 10.1177/0146167207311909.

9. Alexander, C.N., Langer, E.J., Newman, R.I., Chandler, H.M. and Davies, J.L., 'Transcendental meditation, mindfulness, and longevity: An experimental study with the elderly', *Journal of Personality and Social Psychology*, December 1989;57(6):950–64.

10. Langer, E.J., Bashner, R.S. and Chanowitz, B., 'Decreasing prejudice by increasing discrimination', *Journal of Personality and Social Psychology*, July 1985;49(1):113–20.

11. Langer, E.J. and Imber, L.G., 'When practice makes imperfect: Debilitating effects of overlearning', *Journal of Personality and Social Psychology*, 1979, Nov;37(11):2014–24.

12. https://www.meditationcapsules.com/

Chapter 17

1. Brouwers, A. and Tomic, W., 'A longitudinal study of teacher burnout and perceived self efficacy in classroom management', *Teaching and Teacher Education*, 2000;16(2):239–53.

2. Ozdemir, Y., 'The role of classroom management efficacy in predicting teacher burnout', *International Journal of Science in Society*, 2007;2(4):257–63.

Chapter 18

1. Fredrickson, B.L., Cohn, M.A., Coffey, K.A., Pek, J. and Finkel, S.M., 'Open hearts build lives: Positive emotions, induced through loving-kindness meditation, build consequential personal resources', *Journal of Personality and Social Psychology*, 2008;95(5):1045–62.

2. Britton, W.B., Haynes, P.L., Fridel, K.W. and Bootzin, R.R., 'Mindfulness-based cognitive therapy improves polysomnographic and subjective sleep profiles in antidepressant users with sleep complaints', *Psychotherapy and Psychosomatics*; 2012;81(5):296–304.

3. Monshat, K., Khong, B., Hassed, C., Vella-Brodrick, D., Norrish, J., Burns, J. and Herrman, H., '"A conscious control over life and my emotions", Mindfulness practice and healthy young people. A qualitative study,' *Journal of Adolescent Health*, 20 November 2012.

DOI:pii: S1054–139X(12)00400–4. 10.1016/j.jadohealth.2012.09.008.

4. Interested readers are referred to his books *Intimacy and Desire* and *Passionate Marriage*.

5. Grossmann, T., Johnson, M.H., Lloyd-Fox, S., Blasi, A., Deligianni, F., Elwell, C. and Csibra, G., 'Early cortical specialization for face-to-face communication in human infants', *Proceedings of the Royal Society B: Biological Sciences*, 2008;275(1653): 2803–11.

6. Maselko, J., Kubzansky, L., Lipsitt, L. and Buka, S.L., 'Mother's affection at 8 months predicts emotional distress in adulthood', *Journal of Epidemiology and Community Health*, 2010. DOI:10.1136/jech.2009.097873.

7. McGowan, P.O., Sasaki, A., D'Alessio, A.C., et al,. 'Epigenetic regulation of the glucocorticoid receptor in human brain associates with childhood abuse', *Nature Neuroscience*, March 2009;12(3):342–8. DOI:10.1038/nn.2270.

8. Entringer, S., Epel, E.S., Kumsta, R., Lin, J., Hellhammer, D.H., Blackburn, E.H., Wüst, S. and Wadhwa, P.D., 'Stress exposure in intrauterine life is associated with shorter telomere length in young adulthood', *Proceedings of the National Academy of Sciences of the United States of America*, 16 August 2011;108(33):E513–8.

9. Lillard, A.S. and Peterson, J., 'The immediate impact of different types of television on young children's executive function', *Pediatrics*, accessed 12 September 2011. DOI:10.1542/peds.2010–1919.

10. http://www.umassmed.edu/cfm/index.aspx

11. Mathers, C.D. and Loncar, D., 'Projections of global mortality and burden of disease from 2002 to 2030', *PLOS Medicine*, November 2006;3(11):e442.

12. http://monash.edu/counselling/mindfulness.html

13. meditationaustralia.org.au/

14. http://www.meditationinstructors.com/

Chapter 19

1. Rosenthal, J.M. and Okie, S., 'White coat, mood indigo: Depression in medical school', *New England Journal of Medicine*, 2005;353(11):1085–8.

2. http://smilingmind.com.au/

INDEX

A

abstract thinking, capacity for 175
academic performance
    improved memory 61–2
    improving 54
acceptance
    cultivating 92
    of emotions 100–2
    explained 15–7
    house colour analogy 160
    stress reduction 160
    unpleasant thoughts 159–60
    without criticism 99
'accidental' moments 152
'achievement teachers' 37
achieving learning style 36
addictions
    recovering from 33
    to technology 119–20, 142
ADHD
    concentration meditation 59
    executive brain function 41
    'urge surfing' 33
adolescence
    brain development 97
    changing social world 176
    emotional development 174–5
Alzheimer's disease 119
ambiguity 75
Americans, mindfulness trait 188

amygdala 41
anger
    prolonged 98
    riding out 176
anhedonia 46
anterior cingulate cortex (ACC) 24
anxiety
    about teaching performance 144
    effect on performance 74
    upcoming exams 122
applied mindfulness 49–55
assumptions
    recognising 75
    unconscious 69–70
attention
    during communication 104
    divided 63–4
    DLPFC function 24
    improving 57–66
    memory improvement 61–2
    prioritising 8
    redirecting 51–2
    'selective' 70
    surface learners 35
    training 27–8, 58–61
attention deficit trait (ADT) 141, 187
attention regulation 7–9
attention switching 26
'attention training' 171

'attentional blink' 26, 65
attention-seeking behaviour 162
automatic pilot
   'presenteeism' 142
   speaking out of habit 109
   stepping out of 107
   teaching pace 145
avoidance 89–90
awareness
   communicating with, exercise 231–3
   expanding your awareness exercise
     214–8
   tuning in to your surroundings
     exercise 208–14
axe sharpening 58, 61, 92

B
'beginner's mind' 71–2
behaviour
   attention-seeking 162
   in the classroom 162
   unethical/unjust 182
beliefs, unquestioned 70
bias
   anchoring 69
   effect of 69–70
   recognising 75
   unconscious 70–2
Biggs, John 35
biology studies, science of mindfulness
   149
body, caring for 171–2
body scan 60, 134, 164, 195, 200–4
boundaries see limits
brain
   Alzheimer's disease 119
   attention training 27–8
   changes with empathy 111–2
   connections and pathways 21–2
   default mode 22–3
   effect of unmindfulness 47
   executive function 23–6
   hippocampus function 68

overactive stress centre 41
   slowing ageing 119
brain development, adolescence 97
breastfeeding 185
breath counting 60
breathing
   breath as anchor exercise 205–8
   emotional state 164
   during exercise 139
   focusing on 52
   mindful 60
   when overwhelmed 178
bullying 113, 116
burnout 141
businesses, mindfulness programs 189

C
'carer fatigue' 112
catastrophising 18
challenges
   avoidance of 78
   increasing difficulty 73–4
chanting 60
cheating 37
children
   'beginner's mind' 71–2
   creative play 121
   learning inattention 7
   learning process 79
   praised for effort 81
   recognise emotion in faces 184
   teaching them mindfulness 184–5
chronic pain 32
chunking, working memory 63
Churchill, Winston 180
'classical conditioning' 118
classroom
   maintaining discipline 161–3
   managing emotions in 163
   mindfulness introduction 196–7
cognitive control 27
cognitive flexibility, DLPFC function 24
cognitive practices

four main aspects 12–3
perception 13–4
'comma' 12
communication
increasing connection 164–5
with intention 109–10
media forms 190
mindful 104–10
non-verbal 107
online 117–8
poor 46
teaching style 145
unmindful 103, 106–7
compassion
vs empathy 111–2
the golden rule 180
types of 162–3
complacency 142
concentration 136
concentration meditation
common examples 60
explained 58–9
confirmation bias 69
connectedness 114, 126–7, 165
connection, parents with children
184–5, 186
conscience 182
cooperation 114
core principles 181–2
creativity
child's play 121
enhancing 121–9
flow of 126
from stillness 128–9
cricket training accident 135
Csíkszentmihályi, Mihály 28–9
curiosity 101, 140
curriculum, introducing mindfulness
148–50, 191
cyber-bullying 113, 116

D
da Vinci, Leonardo 122, 126

deadlines, managing 93
decision making, ACC function 24
deep learning style 36
'deep teachers' 37–8
default mode 195
denial 89–90
depression, global health issue 187
detachment 14–5
dialectic approach to education 1–2
differentiation 177–8
disappointment, not showing 98–9
discernment 166
discipline, in classroom 161–3
disorganisation 90
distortion, of perception 13–4
distractibility 187
distractions
allowing 46
in the classroom 147–8
common types of 53–4
creative process 126
dealing with 8–9
managing 143
from paying attention 63
recognising 52
'trains of thought' 10
working with, exercise 237–8
writing down 53–4
'divided attention' experiments 26
DIY mindfulness 200
dorsolateral prefrontal cortex (DLPFC) 24
Dweck, Carol 78

E
eating
mindful 9, 50, 172
mindful eating exercise 218–21
education
inside-out approach 1–2
mindfulness approach 2
mindfulness training 188
student's perspective 2
efficiency, achieving 90

ego 137, 180
Einstein, Albert 3, 69, 84, 128, 180–1
elite athletes 136
emails 116–7, 117
emotional development 97–102
emotional intelligence (EQ) 178
'emotional reactivity' 174–5
emotional regulation 98–102
emotional wellbeing, poor 45–6
emotions
    acceptance of 100–2, 159–60
    OFC function 24
    suppressing 99
    suppression of 176
    working mindfully with, exercise
      225–30
    working with 99–102
empathy, vs compassion 111–2
enjoyment, lack of 46
enthusiasm, teaching style 144
environment, for mindful learning 143
Epictetus 86
ESSENCE model 143–4
ethics 179–83
exams
    anxiety about 122
    anxiety during 91
    lead up to 87, 91
    relieving anxiety 92
executive function
    facets of 25
    late development 175–6
    prefrontal cortex 23–6
exercise, regular 131
exercises
    body scan 200–4
    communicating with awareness 231–3
    expanding your awareness 214–8
    mindful eating 218–21
    mindful speaking 231–2
    mindful stretching 223–4
    mindful walking 221–3
    multitasking—communicating 235–6

multitasking—problem solving
    236–7
stress response 224–5
tuning in to your surroundings
    208–14
Using the breath as an anchor 205–8
working mindfully with emotions
    225–30
working with distractions 237–8
expectations
    effect of 11
    managing 93–4, 165–7
    from parents 94
experiences, bound by 14–5
experimentation, inviting 153–4
experiments, mindful classrooms 146–8
expert's mind 72
eyes, closed or open 61

F
face-to-face interaction
    lack of 117–8
    replaced by social media 177
failures
    examination of 154–5
    learning from 94–5, 166–7
feelings, unwanted 9
females
    emotional development 97
    prefrontal cortex development 175
fight or flight response
    stress response 86–7
    symptoms 87
fixed mindset
    changing from 83–4
    in children 81
    mental rigidity 78–9
    negative thoughts 75
    opinions of others 165
    signs of 82
flow state 28–9, 40, 136–8
focus
    concentration meditation 59

DLPFC function 24
on the goal 137
on the present 137
results of 25–6
forgiveness 112–3
Frankl, Viktor 173
'full stop' 11–2
future
conscious thinking of 163–4
imagining 25
not reality 17–9

G
global financial crisis (GFC) 187
goal-directed behaviour, OFC function 24
goals 49–50, 179–83, 183
Goleman, Daniel 178
growth mindset
changing to 83–4
explained 80

H
habits
awareness of 82
changing 82
happiness, three types of 173
Harvard University 192
Hassed mindfulness-based stress-
performance curve 41
health, for resilience 88–91
Health Enhancement Program (HEP) 192
healthcare 189
hearing, vs listening 108
'heartfulness' 163, 171
hedonism 18
'helicopter parents' 125
helicopter teachers 144
high achievers 80
'high allostatic load' 31
hippocampus function 68
'holding on' 14–5
hugs, benefit of 118
hurt, dealing with 112–3

I
If (poem) 95
imagination
believed real 122
capacity for 175
not reality 25
vs vision and insight 122–5
immune system 127
impatience, with creative process 125
impulse control, OFC function 24
inappropriate behaviour, inhibiting 24
inattention 22–3, 30
inquiry 153–4
insanity 128
insight 123
instinctive reflexes 133
intentional behaviour, controlling 24
intentions 49–50
interest, teaching style 144
interference, three main forms 125–6
internet, changing use of 116
interpersonal mindfulness 105
intuition 3

J
Jackson, Phil 136
James, William 5–6
Jordan, Michael 84, 136
judgments 166

K
Kabat-Zinn, Jon 32, 171, 186
'kinesthetic awareness' 131
King, Billie Jean 136
Kipling, Rudyard 95
knowledge retention study 25

L
labels, removal of 154, 167
leadership 189
learning
from failure 94–5
mindful 74–6

out of context 127
by rote 67–8
two types of 67–9
learning styles
achieving learners 36
deep learners 36–7
passive 118
surface 35, 37
letting go 14–5
lie detector tests 182
light bulb moments 123, 124
limbic system 175
limits
blurred boundaries 141–2, 180
exploring your own 139
need for 162
Lincoln, Abraham 58
listening
on autopilot 106–7
vs hearing 108
mindful 60, 106–8
mindful exercise 232
vs rehearsing 178–9
unmindful 106–7
long-term memory
remembering names 64
see also short-term memory
lying, problem of praise 81

M
males
emotional development 97
prefrontal cortex development 175
Man's Search for Meaning (book) 173–4
mantra 58
mantra meditation 60
Marlatt, Alan 33
media
managing 143
social media 116–8, 177
medical students, stress release program 192
meditation

eyes closed or open 61
improved students' retention 25
mantra meditation 58, 60
to punctuate the day 147
responses to word 153
stereotypical notions of 6
two broad types 58
memorising 67–8
memory
academic performance 61–2
extremes of 62
in the hippocampus 68
improving 53, 57–66, 64–6
poor 47
short-term 53
mental flexibility 70–2, 127–8, 146
mental health
conditions aided 189
effect of mindfulness 31, 33
global problems 187
poor 141
mental rehearsal 22
mental rigidity 78–9
mental roadblocks 45
military personnel, mindfulness practices 179
mind, caring for 173
mindfulness
applied 49–55
basic practices 51
benefits of 195
broad focus of 59
classroom introduction 196–7
in classrooms 146–8
common examples 60
cultivating 142–50
in day-to-day life 9–10
defining 6
DIY 200
emotion regulation 98–102
everyday nature of 152
experiments in 147
explaining 6

health-based applications 189
making matters worse 77
memory and 64–6
organic approach 193–4
range of applications 29–33
'mindfulness fatigue' 149, 196
Mindfulness for Academic Success (MAS)
    Monash University 50–5
    written exercise 52–3
mindfulness meditation
    formal practice 10–2, 92, 156
    informal practice 92, 156
mindfulness programs
    HEP 192
    Meditation Capsules 147
    Mindfulness for Academic Success
    (MAS) 50–5
    online and app-based 190
    SRP 192
mindfulness skills, secondary school
    students 101
mindsets
    ability to change 81–2
    choices 83
    hearing internal voice 83
    steps to change 83–4
    subtle 77–8
    see also fixed mindset; growth mindset
'mirror neurons' 111–2
modelling, of teachers 144–5
Monash University
    ESSENCE model 143
    MAS program 50–5
    mindfulness programs 188, 192–3
motivation, lack of 47
movement
    in everyday life 138
    mindful 131–6, 172
    minimal effort 139
    slowing down 133–6, 139
    sporting performance 133
Mozart 123–4
multitasking

appearance of efficiency 91
communicating exercise 235–6
in front of children 141–2
inefficiency of 26–7
lost thinking time 65
problem solving exercise 236–7
speaking to children 185
murder 179–80
music exercise 233–4

N

names, forgetting immediately 64
neurons
    brain nerve cells 21–2
    'mirror neurons' 111–2
    piano practice 22
neuroplasticity 21–2, 23
non-acceptance 88
non-attachment 14–5
non-reactivity 166
novelty 146

O

online bullying 113, 116
open-mindedness 72
openness, encouraging 146
opinions, considered vs held 15
orbitofrontal cortex (OFC) 24
outreach 190
over-planning 125
over-thinking 125
oxytocin 118

P

pacing, and variation 145
pain management 32
parents
    expectations 94
    mindful 184–6
    multitasking 185
    unmindful 183–5
past
    conscious thinking of 163–4

no present existence 17–9
recollectable 25
paying attention
  attention regulation 7–9
  mental chatter distraction 63
  parents'/teachers' lack of 183
  prefrontal cortex 23–6
  ways to practise 65–6
perception
  dictates reaction 100
  distortion of 13–4
  Epictetus 86
  imaginary stressors 13
  is everything 86
  of others 165
  Shakespeare 86
performance
  anxiety about 144
  effect of stress 92
performance anxiety 74
performance-stress relationship 38–40
perspective, working without 90–1
photographic memory 62
piano practice, effect on brain 22
plagiarism 37
planning
  DLPFC function 24
  preparation and 18
Plato 68–9
polygraphs 182
Positive Psychology
  main laws of 165
  types of happiness 173
praise
  for being intelligent 81
  problem of 80–1
  for process or outcome 73–4
prayer 60
pre-conceived ideas *see* beliefs
prefrontal cortex
  clogged with worries 91
  development of 175
  emotional regulation 97–8

key executive functions 24
preparation, unmindful 18
'presence of mind' *see* paying
  attention 17
present moment, is reality 17–9
'presenteeism' 142
primary school, mindfulness steps 150
problem solving
  DLPFC function 24
  mental flexibility 127–8
  methods 71
  mindful 74–6
procrastination 54, 89
projecting onto others 110–1
psychology textbook, first classic 5
public policy 190
'punctuation marks' 11–2
purple house analogy 160

Q
questioning 153–4

R
racism 70
reappraisal 98, 99
reasoning, DLPFC function 24
reflex movements, instinctive 133
rehearsing what to say 178–9
relationships, healthy 110–4
relevance, to different ages/stages
  152–3
research 188
resilience
  developing 167
  in happiness 173
  managing stress 87–95
  things that undermine 88
resistance
  to mindfulness 151–7
  reasons for 155
  respect for 157
  two main forms 43–4
rewards, for process or outcome 72–4

rigidity
   breaking under 88
   cognitive 70–1

S

savant memory 62
Schnarch, David 177
screen time
   discerning use of 143
   effect on brain 119
   safe limit 142
secondary school, mindfulness steps 150
'selective attention' 70
self-awareness, OFC function 24
self-care
   benefits of 143–4, 170
   current examples 169–70
   need for 170
self-consciousness, absence of 137
self-control, sense of 137
self-criticism 53–4, 173
self-discovery, means of 154
self-monitoring 27
Seligman, Martin 173
sense of time, altered 137
senses, tuning into 163–4
setbacks 84
Shakespeare 86
short-term memory
   clogged with worries 91
   DLPFC function 24
   effect of multitasking 65
   forgetting names 64
   prefrontal cortex 62–3
   reduced capacity 42
single-pointedness 59
skills, mindful classrooms 146–8
sleep
   improving quality of 172
   unable to 46
'sleepfulness' *see* unmindfulness
smiling 184
smoking, quitting 172

social development 174–9
social isolation 114, 176–7, 187
social media 116–8, 177
social networking 113
society, mindful 186–90
Socrates 68, 182
'Socratic method,' education 1–2
speech
   inherently limited 109
   mindful 108–9
   mindful speaking exercise 231–2
   speaking out of habit 231–2
spontaneity
   disrupting 125
   teaching style 145
sport, mindful 139–40
sporting performance
   mindful movement 133
   retraining movements 134–5
stillness 129
stress
   barrier to learning 141
   effect on performance 92
   empathy vs compassion 112–3
   lack of focus 90
   pre-exam 13
   during pregnancy 184
   reduction by acceptance 160
   stress response exercise 224–5
   'tyranny of the urgent' 119
   what and why of 85–7
Stress Release Program (SRP) 192
stress response
   body's role 86–7
   effect on brain 30–1
stressors, imaginary 13–4
stress-performance relationship 38–40
stretching, mindful exercise 223–4
students
   pre-exam stress 13
   secondary school 101
studies, negative approach to 100
successes, expressions of 154–5

suppression of emotions 99
surface learning style 35, 37
'surface teachers' 37
sympathetic nervous system 30
Szent-Gyorgyi, Albert 72

T
Tai chi 60
taking for granted 146
teacher burnout 159
teachers, stress of vocation 163–4
teaching mindfully
    major barriers to 141–2
    strategies and tips 142–50
teaching styles 37–8, 144–8
teamwork 114
technology
    addiction to 119–20, 142
    in the bedroom 119
    increasing use of 177
    intentional usage 118
    mindless use of 116
    neither good nor bad 115
    passive learning style 118
    social isolation 177
    as teaching tool 143
    wise use of 120
tension
    effect of lack of 89–90
    habituated to 14–5
    procrastination 89
tertiary education, mindfulness steps 150
texting 177
The Karate Kid (movie) 133–4
The Power of Now (book) 128
the zone 28–9, 40, 136–8
thinking, DLPFC function 24
'thought labelling' 52
thoughts
    acceptance of 159–60
    choosing 161–2
    cruel or unfair 179–80
    distance from 102

expectations 94
    of failure 95
    fixed mindset 75
    identification with 78–9
    negative 78–9
    observing 33
    trying to get rid of 153
    unwanted 9
time, sense altered 137
time management, deadlines 93
'time out' 102
time wasting 45, 89–90
Tolle, Eckhart 128
training programs 188
'trains of thought' *see* distractions
'tyranny of the urgent' 119

U
understanding 45
unmindfulness
    costs of 43–7, 195
    costs to individual 186
    costs to society 186–7
    default mode 195
    effect on brain 47
    generational problem 183
    listening and communication 103,
        106–7
'urge surfing' 33

V
values 174, 179–83
vision
    explained 123
    translating into reality 125–6

W
walking
    baby's learning process 79
    learning process 132–3
    mindful 9, 134
    mindful exercise 221–3
    slower pace 171–2

wasting time 45, 89–90
working memory *see* short-term memory
work-life balance 141–2, 143–4
workload, ways we increase 88–91
worry, poses as preparation 9–10, 18

Y
Yerkes-Dodson stress-performance curve 39
yoga 60

DR STEPHEN MCKENZIE

co-author of the bestselling *Mindfulness for Life*

mindfulness
AT WORK

How to avoid stress,
achieve more and enjoy life!

An extract from *Mindfulness at Work* by Dr Stephen McKenzie, also published by Exisle Publishing, and available from: www.exislepublishing.com

CHAPTER 9

Mindfulness and our life work

Enjoy your achievements as well as your plans.
Keep interested in your own career, however humble;
it is a real possession in the changing fortunes of time.

Desiderata (reputedly found in St Paul's Church, Baltimore, 1692; actually written by Max Ehrmann, 1927)

Most of us spend most of our time doing some kind of work, whether we like it or not. Work is a vital aspect of our lives and it can also be our greatest opportunity to achieve a profound working knowledge and to experience the complete peace and enjoyment that comes when we work out who we really are: connected, fulfilled and happy. There's more to our working whole than the sum of our working parts, and we can realise the deeper value of work to our whole being when we realise that we don't work just to live, but also live to work … on ourselves. This doesn't mean that we were born to be whatever it is that we're working at — whether that's a dishwasher, a tax accountant, a camel jockey or whatever — but that whatever we're working at gives us a unique opportunity to go beyond it to find out what we're really working at and who we really are.

What really works for us?

Our jobs can do much more for us and for the people we're connected with than just help us to pay our household bills (enormously helpful though this might be!). Our jobs can also help us to pay our cosmic bills — repaying our individual life investment by re-connecting to its source. Our real work isn't what we do in our jobs; it's what we do in ourselves, and once we work out who we really are it's relatively easy to find out what job works best for us and how to best do it.

To do any job as well and as rewardingly as we can, we need to understand a greater practical reality than just how we can work best at a mechanical level, and we need to understand a greater human reality than just who we think we are. Our greater reality consists of the total picture of all the people and situations and events that we experience, and not just the bits of the picture that we're fleetingly interested in. Psychologists like to show people stuff that they think helps them think, but at least some of the stuff that psychologists like to show people can help them to do more than just think, it can help them to *know*.

A gestalt is a picture that we can perceive in different ways; a well-known example is a picture that is either of an old woman or a young woman wearing a scarf depending on how we see it or work it out. It's the same picture, but how we see it can change. A common working example of a gestalt is when something happens that we call an interruption to our work. Because we've seen what happened as 'an interruption', this is the picture of it that we've created. We could also see the situation as a welcome opportunity to do something unexpected and valuable, and possibly as a welcome opportunity to help someone who needs our help. The real meaning of any gestalt, including human life and human working life, is that our answer is the total picture, not just the bits of it that we're stuck on.

Our true working reality, like our true living reality, includes not just our big picture but our *huge* picture — of all the people and situations to which we are connected, including our customers, colleagues, underlings and even our bosses! Our work gives us a vital opportunity to reach a higher and more connected consciousness, which gives us a macro life and working-life perspective far greater than the micro perspectives than can upset us so much.

Small picture workplace catastrophes such as hammering our thumbnail instead of our gang nail, or putting antelope rather than cantaloupe in the vegetarians' fruit salad, don't *force* us to get upset. They just give us an *opportunity* to get upset. We can choose to rise above our attachments to what only *looks like* our ultimate reality, and instead do the opposite of getting upset. With the right mindfulness set our jobs are a portal to an unshakeable understanding of our life, our work and our life work as something deeply right and valuable. With the right mindfulness set we can see ourselves as an integral part of a vast working whole rather than just a working pimple that wants to be promoted to a boil. Our jobs are a wonderful opportunity for us to see our particular place in the magnificent cosmic creation and they are constantly flashing cosmic connection messages at us in neon lights … if we take off our mind-made dark glasses and just see the light: 'You are here! You are now! This is it!'

Working mindfulness can help us to understand not only where we are and who we are, but also where we are going and why.

Working our way to enlightenment

In Pali, the language of Gautama the Buddha, *Dhamma* means 'The Way of Truth'. This word is spelled *Dharma* in the Sanskrit language, but however we spell it or pronounce or define it, the ability to find our natural and right way and follow it is vital to our life success and to our working-life success. We can't follow someone else's natural and right way and expect to find our home base of natural peace and fulfilment and optimal productivity. We can't beg, borrow or steal. We can only recognise it and our own way there, and follow it. When referring to *Dhamma*, the spiritual teacher Eknath Easwaran wrote: 'In the sphere of human activity probably no word is richer in its connotations. Dharma is behavior that is in line with … unity.'[1]

Would you rather get a fabulous pay rise that would allow you to buy a new house or spouse so seemingly irresistible that other people will envy it, or would you rather get nothing more than what you have right now — on the outside — but have so much peace and contentment and joy on the inside that you don't care if you have any more external stuff or not or care what anyone else thinks? This is what enlightenment is. Or if you prefer a psychological term for the same state rather than a spiritual one, then try on for size the psychologist Abraham Maslow's well-known term *self-actualisation*. Both words mean the same thing: actually finding our real self and then actualising it — doing something with it, working with it, lighting up with the joy of it.

Being enlightened or self-actualised or permanently at peace and happy without an external reason doesn't mean we have to take off to a cave and feel smug there about having what most people don't. There's actually something extremely practical about being in a state of 'beyond mind' because in it we break into life's real value, rather than unsuccessfully trying to break out of its opposite. In our natural, ultimately mindful state we know ourselves so completely that we also know others completely, and we are highly valuable to others as well as to ourselves. Working enlightenment is a much greater and more valuable thing than theoretical enlightenment, and we can work our way towards it by freeing ourselves of our mind-made distractions and treating our present work, whatever it is, as a gift. Being mindful can help us to unwrap our working gifts by helping us to recognise that something wrapped up in plain brown lunch paper or plain work clothes can be far greater than something wrapped up in the glitter of expectations.

The first simple but profound steps towards the mind- and heart-broadening possibilities of employing mindfulness at work are:

- Being aware and accepting of what we are working on, no matter what we think.
- Treating others as we would like to be treated, no matter what we think of them.
- Helping ourselves work towards where we need to get by helping others work towards where they need to get.

A consequence and also a driver of our mindful oiling of our rusty working parts is that as our working state of consciousness progresses so does our working conscience. In higher states of working mindfulness we are less likely to rationalise our working life dysfunctions, such as by attempting to justify work practices that benefit our interests at the expense of other people's interests. In higher states of working consciousness we are less likely to think that our working ends justify our working means. There might indeed be a sucker born every minute, as the American showman P.T. Barnum once noted. A mindful and heartful attitude to our work, however, will help us to realise that the real suckers are those of us who don't realise our connectedness, and who try to profit from the equivalent of their left hand pulling the wool over their right eye.

If the huge practical benefits of working mindfulness still sound idealistic or esoteric or a long way off or like something that will work only for other people, then please try a simple thought experiment. Think of a situation when you worked mindfully — with full attention and acceptance — and now think of one when you didn't, when you were distracted from what you were doing by what you would have liked to be doing … Which situation felt better, once your ego tidal wave subsided far enough to expose your universal reason?

What does an enlightened workplace look like?

It might seem like the only enlightened workplaces are monasteries up mountains, but there are actually some very ordinary examples of some very extraordinary and extraordinarily high profile people who have incorporated some enlightened work practices and possibilities into their organisations. Richard Branson, founder and chairman of the Virgin Group, helped to start a worldwide council of Elders that aims to bring some practical sanity into the working world. Australian entrepreneur Dick Smith has introduced large-scale lines of local products with a local conscience into supermarkets despite fierce opposition from competitors. Oprah Winfrey made much more than just fame and billions of dollars by publicly championing people she believed in to far greater acceptance and influence than they would have achieved without her help, including minority groups, Barack Obama and Eckhart Tolle.

When we work mindfully, our minds and our hearts open out to the ultimate reality of our human situation — and this means the ultimate working reality of who we are really connected to, what we are really working on, and how to really get the best working outcome for everyone. No matter how big we think the organisation we work for is, what we are really working for is The Universe Inc. When we work mindfully we can realise that nobody lives or works alone, no matter what we think. Even if we think that we are the most dispensable employee of Harry's Fish and Chip Emporium, or the most senior employer at Manangatang Megamarketing Inc., we are all working this life shift together.

Working mindfully works because it helps us to work more successfully and enjoyably. Mindfulness is just a word that describes what we already have: a life essence and a life purpose. Now it's time to put this book down and put your thoughts about it away — filed under 'F' for finished. Now it's time to stop 'working' and just *do*, now. And just *be*, always.

1. Easwaran, E., *The Dhammapada*, Blue Mountain Center of Meditation, 1987, p. 24.

Mindfulness for Life

DR STEPHEN MCKENZIE AND DR CRAIG HASSED

Written by two experts with many years of personal and clinical experience, *Mindfulness for Life* is designed to be your complete guide to living a more mindful life. Whether you want to:

- reduce stress and anxiety
- reduce your risk of disease
- overcome addiction
- unhook yourself from depression
- manage your weight
- perform better at work
- be a better parent
- or simply enjoy a good night's sleep …

mindfulness can help! Only a few minutes a day can start to change your life.

> *'Do read this book. Do give it to someone you care about …*
> *Mindfulness works!'*
>
> **Ian Gawler, OAM**

ISBN 978 1 921966 03 3

 **e-newsletter**

If you love books as much as we do, why not subscribe
to our weekly e-newsletter?

As a subscriber, you'll receive special offers and discounts,
be the first to hear of our exciting upcoming titles, and
be kept up to date with book tours and author events.
You will also receive unique opportunities exclusive
to subscribers – and much more!

To subscribe in Australia or from any other
country except New Zealand, visit
www.exislepublishing.com.au/newsletter-sign-up

For New Zealand, visit
www.exislepublishing.co.nz/newsletter-subscribe